SPOT CHECK

AllergySafeCertification

Allergy Safe Certification Training Manual

Lynn L. Bolgen • Brenda D. Vasser
Spot Check, Inc.
PO Box 22051
Seattle, WA 98122
206-568-7134

Digit on the right indicates the number of this printing: 200905205
Second Printing/Updated May 2014

Library of Congress Control Number: TXu1-700-790
ISBN: 978-0-615-38516-7

Cover photographs copyright 2011 by Spot Check, Inc.
Book cover and interior design by Spot Check, Inc.
Printing and print layout design by LaserWriting, Tacoma, Washington.
Photography credits — LaserWriting: John Leach, David Petersen and Fajr Wilson
Thanks to Swiftwater Cellars for allowing us to photograph their staff and premises.
301 Rope Rider Dr., Cle Elum, Washington • 509.674.6555

This book may be ordered by mail from the publisher.
Please include $9.95 for postage and handling.

Spot Check, Inc.
PO Box 22051
Seattle, Washington 98122
Visit us on the web!
www.spotck.com

ALLERGY SAFE CERTIFICATION
TABLE OF CONTENTS

1. INTRODUCTION 4

2. WHY IS THIS TRAINING IMPORTANT TO MY
   ORGANIZATION AND TO ME? 6

3. FOOD ALLERGY LAWS AND REGULATIONS 8
   a. Food Allergen Labeling and Consumer Protection Act of 2004
   b. FDA FOOD CODE
      — FDA
   c. ONTARIO LEGISLATIVE ASSEMBLY BILL 3
      — Sabrina's Law

4. WHAT IS A FOOD ALLERGY? 25

5. CASE STUDIES
   a. JASON (Milk) 36
   b. JOHN (Egg) 39
   c. DAVID (Peanut) 42
   d. JOANNE (Tree Nut) 45
   e. HEATHER (Fin Fish) 48
   f. LESLIE (Shell Fish) 51
   g. TAMMY (Wheat) 53
   h. JIM (Soy) 56
   I. ALLEN (Sesame) 59
   i. BRENDA 61
   j. LYNN 63
   k. RESTAURANT 65

6. FOOD HANDLING RESPONSIBILITIES FOR:
   a. INDIVIDUAL 68
   b. HOST OR HOSTESS 71
   c. BUS PERSON 74
   d. SERVER 77
   e. DISH WASHER 82
   f. CHEF 85
   g. MANAGER 90

7. COMMON SOURCES OF FOOD ALLERGY CONTAMINATION 94

8. CRITICAL ELEMENTS OF A SUCCESSFUL FOOD ALLERGY PROGRAM 98

9. RESOURCES AND REFERENCES 100

10. FOOD ALLERGY SAFE TRAINER'S GUIDE 101

INTRODUCTION

The average human will consume from 700 to 1,000 tons of food in their lifetime. Much of this food will be purchased from restaurants, delis, bakeries, school cafeterias and other public or private food establishments, with busy schedules and long commutes more and more families are eating foods prepared outside the home. This practice increases the opportunity for individuals with food allergies, food intolerances, and food sensitivities to accidentally encounter more of the offending foods in establishments. When we make mistakes due to lack of knowledge, protocols, policies, procedures or indifference, they are either sick or dead.

The Scientific Community

Current estimates by the scientific community tell us that between 2.5 and 4% of the U.S. population have food allergies and an additional 10 to 25% suffer from food intolerances and food sensitivities. Estimates in Canada reflect that 2% of adult population and between 3 and 8% of children suffer from food allergies, with the incidences of food intolerances and sensitivities ranging from 10 to 30% of the population. Based on the Canada statistics from March 2010 population numbers of 34,060,000 equates to a minimum of 4,087,200 and a maximum of 10,218,000 individuals who have some sort of negative physical reaction to one or more foods.

INTRODUCTION

The estimates for England are even higher with 30 to 50% of the population suffering from food allergies, intolerances or sensitivities. The Office for National Statistics 2008 national population projections of 51,460,000 equate to between 15,438,000 and 25,730,000 individuals who have some sort of negative physical reaction to one or more foods. The U.S. Census Bureau's 2008 estimated population of 303,824,650 equates to minimally 45,573,698 individuals who have some sort of a negative physical reaction to one or more foods.

With numbers of this magnitude we in the food service industry are compelled to do all we can to ensure the health and safety of this large segment of the public. Statistics indicate that over 50,000 individuals visit emergency rooms each year for food allergy reactions alone and that over 200 of these people will die as a result of their reaction. An additional 125,000+ will visit local clinics or private physicians. These numbers do not include the individuals who seek medical treatment for food intolerances or food sensitivities. More importantly, many emergency room physicians state that food allergy, food intolerance and food sensitivity issues are "grossly under reported," and that the real number of these cases is "substantially higher."

What We Know

What we do know and experts can confirm is that food allergy, food intolerances and food sensitivity cases are rapidly increasing. Currently, for all allergic reactions treated in emergency rooms today, food is the leading cause. Medical costs associated with this issue are in the billions and someone is going to bear the growing expense.

As an industry we can do our part to prevent or greatly reduce incidents of food-related reactions through education and enlightened food handling. We must establish protocols, processes and procedures within our facilities that will protect our guests. We must become a part of the solution, not the problem.

Our Liability

Our industry is seeing increased lawsuits, insurance claims and public complaints. Our liability becomes greater as law makers, courts and the public demand we educate our staff and implement protocols, policies and procedures to safeguard our guests.

Every time the public learns of someone made sick or killed by our lack of knowledge and/or protocol, policies and procedures, we as an industry lose public trust. Along with the individuals and families who are damaged, some irreparably, our reputations as owners, business people, corporate citizens, employees and as an industry are severely tarnished.

WHY IS THIS TRAINING IMPORTANT TO MY ORGANIZATION AND TO ME?

With over 45,000,000 food-challenged customers in the U.S., 10,000,000 in Canada and 25,000,000 in England we literally and figuratively cannot afford to turn these individuals away. This means, in more manageable terms, that nearly two out of every ten people who walk through our doors have some sort of food issue. We are presented with the unique opportunity to contribute to public health and create a safe dining environment for these individuals.

When we create a food allergy safe establishment we literally put out the welcome mat for these guests, and of course since they do not dine alone we welcome everyone in their party. Conversely, when we are unable to accommodate individuals with food allergies, food sensitivities and food intolerances we turn away their families, friends and business colleagues.

Study after study show food-challenged individuals and individuals with food-challenged friends and families will frequent establishments that will accommodate their needs. When we accommodate these needs we create strong loyalties and repeat business, we also know these individuals will exercise their insistence, recommending and suggesting our establishments to those within their sphere of influence.

Blue Ginger chef-owner Ming Tsai, who is also a national spokesman for Food Allergy and Anaphylaxis Network, has created an elaborate system at his Wellesley, Massachusetts, restaurant to accommodate people with allergies. When a customer with a food allergy asks about a dish, the server checks the restaurant's Food Bible, a binder that contains every menu item with every ingredient and highlights any food allergens. Then the server asks Tsai or the manager whether the dish can be made safely. The server prints out a meal ticket with red type indicating that this is a food allergy meal and highlights the ticket with a marker. Tsai or the manager on duty initials the ticket, which stays next to the plate until it is served.

Tsai, whose six-year-old son David has several life-threatening food allergies, said businesses in the hospitality industry have an obligation to serve everyone. But even he's been turned away from restaurants that don't want to take the risk of serving his son. "People used to discriminate based on the skin color and wheelchairs. Nowadays there is discrimination against people with food allergies," Tsai said. "But creating policies to accommodate people with food allergies isn't going to put restaurants out of business. It's going to save lives." *

* From the text – On the Nature of Food Allergy

WHY IS THIS TRAINING IMPORTANT TO MY ORGANIZATION AND TO ME?

Valued Employee

In short, not only is Food Allergy Safe Training the right and responsible thing to do, it also makes dollars and sense. By taking this class and obtaining the Food Allergy Safe Certification you become a more effective and valuable employee.

The Certified Team

When your entire team is Food Allergy Safe Certified, you make each responsible and can hold each accountable for the proper handling of food allergy issues which ensures a standard knowledge base for all employees.

You are assured that every staff member who comes in contact with a guest or their food knows exactly what to do and how to handle that guest's food allergy issues and needs. When all staff is Food Allergy Safe Certified you know the depth of knowledge of every team members training in food allergy handling protocols, policies and procedures.

The more trained and certified staff you have the safer your guests and your organization.

With all staff members trained and certified, you create an individual and team approach to food allergy safety.

Food Allergy Safe Certified establishments assure those 45,000,000 in the U.S., 10,000,000 in Canada and 25,000,000 in England who are food-allergic, food-sensitive and food-intolerant individuals that you and your staff have a high understanding of their issues and can be trusted to safely handle their food issues. Their friends, families and business associates will also learn of your concern for the public's health.

FOOD ALLERGY LAWS AND REGULATIONS

FEDERAL PUBLIC LAW 108-282
Food Allergen Labeling and Consumer Protection Act of 2004

FEDERAL PUBLIC LAW 108-282 August 2, 2004. Known as the Food Allergen Labeling and Consumer Protection Act of 2004, passed by the U.S. Senate March 9, 2004 and passed by the House of Representatives July 29, 2004.

This Act studied the issue of food labeling and consumer protection as it pertains to all aspects of food handling. This includes manufacturing through food establishments, restaurants, grocery store delicatessens, delicatessens, bakeries, elementary school and secondary school cafeterias.

Section 209 Food Allergens in the Food Code of the Food Allergen Labeling and Consumer Protection Act deals specifically with the food service industry.

This section states: "The Secretary (Secretary of Health and Human Services) shall consider guidelines and recommendations developed by the public and private entities for public and private food establishments for preparing allergen free foods in pursuing this revision." This language has been interpreted by the "experts" to mean that if we as an industry do not demonstrate "voluntary" compliance we will go the way of the manufacturing industry and be **subject to mandatory regulations.**

FOOD ALLERGY LAWS AND REGULATIONS

The Public Law provided a period (18 months was spent) to investigate food labeling, and found that 25% of the food labels reviewed had food allergens that were either not "clearly labeled" or were not disclosed at all!

As a result, on January 1, 2006 compliance with the Federal Law went from voluntary to mandatory for manufacturers. The Federal guidelines had to be met by all manufacturers by December 31, 2008.

Since this legislation's inception in 2004, we as an industry have taken the following position: we were so hampered by inadequate food labeling that effective and comprehensive allergy safe food handling was next to impossible. We were effectively in the same position as the general public; we had to be experts in chemistry to figure out the many names given to the ingredients listed on packaging.

Federal legislators agreed and have allowed our industry some grace until manufacturing caught up with the law. The legislators gave manufacturers until December 31, 2008 to list in plain language the **"Big 8 Allergens"** on their labels.

Effective January 1, 2009 our industry cannot claim we can't act because we don't know. Some states have already enacted legislation to bolster the Food Allergen Labeling and Consumer Protection Act and many more are in the beginning stages of introducing new legislation which will impact the food service industry. As allergy expert Dr. Paul J. Hannaway states, "The thrust of all this legislative activity is that food service providers must train their managers, chefs, kitchen and wait-staff about the risks posed by food allergies. This responsibility applies not only to restaurants, but to bakeries, coffee and donut shops, delicatessens, commercial airlines, cruise ships, ice cream shops, hospitals, camps, college cafeterias and food caterers—in other words anyone involved in serving the general public."

If our industry does not demonstrate our willingness to self regulate and voluntarily comply in a very public and noticeable fashion, then, just as manufacturers were, our industry will be **forced** to comply. This affords us a short window of opportunity to institute effective food allergy safe protocols, policies and procedures.

(T) Section 108(b)(3) of Public Law 90–399 is amended by striking "section 201(w) as added by this Act" and inserting "section 201(v)".

21 USC 360b note.

(6) REGULATIONS.—On the date of enactment of this Act, the Secretary of Health and Human Services shall implement sections 571 and 573 of the Federal Food, Drug, and Cosmetic Act and subsequently publish implementing regulations. Not later than 12 months after the date of enactment of this Act, the Secretary shall issue proposed regulations to implement section 573 of the Federal Food, Drug, and Cosmetic Act (as added by this Act), and not later than 24 months after the date of enactment of this Act, the Secretary shall issue final regulations implementing section 573 of the Federal Food, Drug, and Cosmetic Act. Not later than 18 months after the date of enactment of this Act, the Secretary shall issue proposed regulations to implement section 572 of the Federal Food, Drug, and Cosmetic Act (as added by this Act), and not later than 36 months after the date of enactment of this Act, the Secretary shall issue final regulations implementing section 572 of the Federal Food, Drug, and Cosmetic Act. Not later than 30 months after the date of enactment of this Act, the Secretary shall issue proposed regulations to implement section 571 of the Federal Food, Drug, and Cosmetic Act (as added by this Act), and not later than 42 months after the date of enactment of this Act, the Secretary shall issue final regulations implementing section 571 of the Federal Food, Drug, and Cosmetic Act. These timeframes shall be extended by 12 months for each fiscal year, in which the funds authorized to be appropriated under subsection (i) are not in fact appropriated.

Effective date. Deadlines. Publication. 21 USC 360ccc note.

(7) OFFICE.—The Secretary of Health and Human Services shall establish within the Center for Veterinary Medicine (of the Food and Drug Administration), an Office of Minor Use and Minor Species Animal Drug Development that reports directly to the Director of the Center for Veterinary Medicine. This office shall be responsible for overseeing the development and legal marketing of new animal drugs for minor uses and minor species. There is authorized to be appropriated to carry out this subsection $1,200,000 for fiscal year 2004 and such sums as may be necessary for each fiscal year thereafter.

Government organization. 21 USC 393 note.

Appropriation authorization.

(8) AUTHORIZATION OF APPROPRIATIONS.—There is authorized to be appropriated to carry out section 573(b) of the Federal Food, Drug, and Cosmetic Act (as added by this section) $1,000,000 for the fiscal year following publication of final implementing regulations, $2,000,000 for the subsequent fiscal year, and such sums as may be necessary for each fiscal year thereafter.

TITLE II—FOOD ALLERGEN LABELING AND CONSUMER PROTECTION

Food Allergen Labeling and Consumer Protection Act of 2004. 21 USC 301 note.

SEC. 201. SHORT TITLE.

This title may be cited as the "Food Allergen Labeling and Consumer Protection Act of 2004".

SEC. 202. FINDINGS.

21 USC 343 note.

Congress finds that—

(1) it is estimated that—

(A) approximately 2 percent of adults and about 5 percent of infants and young children in the United States suffer from food allergies; and

(B) each year, roughly 30,000 individuals require emergency room treatment and 150 individuals die because of allergic reactions to food;

(2)(A) eight major foods or food groups—milk, eggs, fish, Crustacean shellfish, tree nuts, peanuts, wheat, and soybeans—account for 90 percent of food allergies;

(B) at present, there is no cure for food allergies; and

(C) a food allergic consumer must avoid the food to which the consumer is allergic;

(3)(A) in a review of the foods of randomly selected manufacturers of baked goods, ice cream, and candy in Minnesota and Wisconsin in 1999, the Food and Drug Administration found that 25 percent of sampled foods failed to list peanuts or eggs as ingredients on the food labels; and

(B) nationally, the number of recalls because of unlabeled allergens rose to 121 in 2000 from about 35 a decade earlier;

(4) a recent study shows that many parents of children with a food allergy were unable to correctly identify in each of several food labels the ingredients derived from major food allergens;

(5)(A) ingredients in foods must be listed by their "common or usual name";

(B) in some cases, the common or usual name of an ingredient may be unfamiliar to consumers, and many consumers may not realize the ingredient is derived from, or contains, a major food allergen; and

(C) in other cases, the ingredients may be declared as a class, including spices, flavorings, and certain colorings, or are exempt from the ingredient labeling requirements, such as incidental additives; and

(6)(A) celiac disease is an immune-mediated disease that causes damage to the gastrointestinal tract, central nervous system, and other organs;

(B) the current recommended treatment is avoidance of glutens in foods that are associated with celiac disease; and

(C) a multicenter, multiyear study estimated that the prevalence of celiac disease in the United States is 0.5 to 1 percent of the general population.

SEC. 203. FOOD LABELING; REQUIREMENT OF INFORMATION REGARDING ALLERGENIC SUBSTANCES.

(a) IN GENERAL.—Section 403 of the Federal Food, Drug, and Cosmetic Act (21 U.S.C. 343) is amended by adding at the end the following:

"(w)(1) If it is not a raw agricultural commodity and it is, or it contains an ingredient that bears or contains, a major food allergen, unless either—

"(A) the word 'Contains', followed by the name of the food source from which the major food allergen is derived, is printed immediately after or is adjacent to the list of ingredients (in a type size no smaller than the type size used in the list of ingredients) required under subsections (g) and (i); or

"(B) the common or usual name of the major food allergen in the list of ingredients required under subsections (g) and (i) is followed in parentheses by the name of the food source from which the major food allergen is derived, except that the name of the food source is not required when—

"(i) the common or usual name of the ingredient uses the name of the food source from which the major food allergen is derived; or

"(ii) the name of the food source from which the major food allergen is derived appears elsewhere in the ingredient list, unless the name of the food source that appears elsewhere in the ingredient list appears as part of the name of a food ingredient that is not a major food allergen under section 201(qq)(2)(A) or (B).

"(2) As used in this subsection, the term 'name of the food source from which the major food allergen is derived' means the name described in section 201(qq)(1); provided that in the case of a tree nut, fish, or Crustacean shellfish, the term 'name of the food source from which the major food allergen is derived' means the name of the specific type of nut or species of fish or Crustacean shellfish.

"(3) The information required under this subsection may appear in labeling in lieu of appearing on the label only if the Secretary finds that such other labeling is sufficient to protect the public health. A finding by the Secretary under this paragraph (including any change in an earlier finding under this paragraph) is effective upon publication in the Federal Register as a notice.

Federal Register, publication.

"(4) Notwithstanding subsection (g), (i), or (k), or any other law, a flavoring, coloring, or incidental additive that is, or that bears or contains, a major food allergen shall be subject to the labeling requirements of this subsection.

"(5) The Secretary may by regulation modify the requirements of subparagraph (A) or (B) of paragraph (1), or eliminate either the requirement of subparagraph (A) or the requirements of subparagraph (B) of paragraph (1), if the Secretary determines that the modification or elimination of the requirement of subparagraph (A) or the requirements of subparagraph (B) is necessary to protect the public health.

"(6)(A) Any person may petition the Secretary to exempt a food ingredient described in section 201(qq)(2) from the allergen labeling requirements of this subsection.

"(B) The Secretary shall approve or deny such petition within 180 days of receipt of the petition or the petition shall be deemed denied, unless an extension of time is mutually agreed upon by the Secretary and the petitioner.

"(C) The burden shall be on the petitioner to provide scientific evidence (including the analytical method used to produce the evidence) that demonstrates that such food ingredient, as derived by the method specified in the petition, does not cause an allergic response that poses a risk to human health.

"(D) A determination regarding a petition under this paragraph shall constitute final agency action.

"(E) The Secretary shall promptly post to a public site all petitions received under this paragraph within 14 days of receipt and the Secretary shall promptly post the Secretary's response to each.

Public information. Deadline.

"(7)(A) A person need not file a petition under paragraph (6) to exempt a food ingredient described in section 201(qq)(2) from the allergen labeling requirements of this subsection, if the person files with the Secretary a notification containing—

"(i) scientific evidence (including the analytical method used) that demonstrates that the food ingredient (as derived by the method specified in the notification, where applicable) does not contain allergenic protein; or

"(ii) a determination by the Secretary that the ingredient does not cause an allergic response that poses a risk to human health under a premarket approval or notification program under section 409.

Deadlines.

"(B) The food ingredient may be introduced or delivered for introduction into interstate commerce as a food ingredient that is not a major food allergen 90 days after the date of receipt of the notification by the Secretary, unless the Secretary determines within the 90-day period that the notification does not meet the requirements of this paragraph, or there is insufficient scientific evidence to determine that the food ingredient does not contain allergenic protein or does not cause an allergenic response that poses a risk to human health.

Public information. Deadline.

"(C) The Secretary shall promptly post to a public site all notifications received under this subparagraph within 14 days of receipt and promptly post any objections thereto by the Secretary.

"(x) Notwithstanding subsection (g), (i), or (k), or any other law, a spice, flavoring, coloring, or incidental additive that is, or that bears or contains, a food allergen (other than a major food allergen), as determined by the Secretary by regulation, shall be disclosed in a manner specified by the Secretary by regulation.".

21 USC 343 note.

(b) EFFECT ON OTHER AUTHORITY.—The amendments made by this section that require a label or labeling for major food allergens do not alter the authority of the Secretary of Health and Human Services under the Federal Food, Drug, and Cosmetic Act (21 U.S.C. 301 et seq.) to require a label or labeling for other food allergens.

(c) CONFORMING AMENDMENTS.—

(1) Section 201 of the Federal Food, Drug, and Cosmetic Act (21 U.S.C. 321) (as amended by section 102(b)) is amended by adding at the end the following:

"(qq) The term 'major food allergen' means any of the following:

"(1) Milk, egg, fish (e.g., bass, flounder, or cod), Crustacean shellfish (e.g., crab, lobster, or shrimp), tree nuts (e.g., almonds, pecans, or walnuts), wheat, peanuts, and soybeans.

"(2) A food ingredient that contains protein derived from a food specified in paragraph (1), except the following:

"(A) Any highly refined oil derived from a food specified in paragraph (1) and any ingredient derived from such highly refined oil.

"(B) A food ingredient that is exempt under paragraph (6) or (7) of section 403(w).".

(2) Section 403A(a)(2) of the Federal Food, Drug, and Cosmetic Act (21 U.S.C. 343–1(a)(2)) is amended by striking "or 403(i)(2)" and inserting "403(i)(2), 403(w), or 403(x)".

Applicability. 21 USC 321 note.

(d) EFFECTIVE DATE.—The amendments made by this section shall apply to any food that is labeled on or after January 1, 2006.

SEC. 204. REPORT ON FOOD ALLERGENS.

Not later than 18 months after the date of enactment of this Act, the Secretary of Health and Human Services (in this section referred to as the "Secretary") shall submit to the Committee on Health, Education, Labor, and Pensions of the Senate and the Committee on Energy and Commerce of the House of Representatives a report that—

(1)(A) analyzes—

(i) the ways in which foods, during manufacturing and processing, are unintentionally contaminated with major food allergens, including contamination caused by the use by manufacturers of the same production line to produce both products for which major food allergens are intentional ingredients and products for which major food allergens are not intentional ingredients; and

(ii) the ways in which foods produced on dedicated production lines are unintentionally contaminated with major food allergens; and

(B) estimates how common the practices described in subparagraph (A) are in the food industry, with breakdowns by food type as appropriate;

(2) advises whether good manufacturing practices or other methods can be used to reduce or eliminate cross-contact of foods with the major food allergens;

(3) describes—

(A) the various types of advisory labeling (such as labeling that uses the words "may contain") used by food producers;

(B) the conditions of manufacture of food that are associated with the various types of advisory labeling; and

(C) the extent to which advisory labels are being used on food products;

(4) describes how consumers with food allergies or the caretakers of consumers would prefer that information about the risk of cross-contact be communicated on food labels as determined by using appropriate survey mechanisms;

(5) states the number of inspections of food manufacturing and processing facilities conducted in the previous 2 years and describes—

(A) the number of facilities and food labels that were found to be in compliance or out of compliance with respect to cross-contact of foods with residues of major food allergens and the proper labeling of major food allergens;

(B) the nature of the violations found; and

(C) the number of voluntary recalls, and their classifications, of foods containing undeclared major food allergens; and

(6) assesses the extent to which the Secretary and the food industry have effectively addressed cross-contact issues.

SEC. 205. INSPECTIONS RELATING TO FOOD ALLERGENS.   21 USC 374a.

The Secretary of Health and Human Services shall conduct inspections consistent with the authority under section 704 of the Federal Food, Drug, and Cosmetic Act (21 U.S.C. 374) of facilities in which foods are manufactured, processed, packed, or held—

(1) to ensure that the entities operating the facilities comply with practices to reduce or eliminate cross-contact of a food

with residues of major food allergens that are not intentional ingredients of the food; and

(2) to ensure that major food allergens are properly labeled on foods.

Deadlines.
Regulations.
21 USC 343 note.

SEC. 206. GLUTEN LABELING.

Not later than 2 years after the date of enactment of this Act, the Secretary of Health and Human Services, in consultation with appropriate experts and stakeholders, shall issue a proposed rule to define, and permit use of, the term "gluten-free" on the labeling of foods. Not later than 4 years after the date of enactment of this Act, the Secretary shall issue a final rule to define, and permit use of, the term "gluten-free" on the labeling of foods.

42 USC 242r.

SEC. 207. IMPROVEMENT AND PUBLICATION OF DATA ON FOOD-RELATED ALLERGIC RESPONSES.

(a) IN GENERAL.—The Secretary of Health and Human Services, acting through the Director of the Centers for Disease Control and Prevention and in consultation with the Commissioner of Food and Drugs, shall improve (including by educating physicians and other health care providers) the collection of, and publish as it becomes available, national data on—

(1) the prevalence of food allergies;

(2) the incidence of clinically significant or serious adverse events related to food allergies; and

(3) the use of different modes of treatment for and prevention of allergic responses to foods.

(b) AUTHORIZATION OF APPROPRIATIONS.—For the purpose of carrying out this section, there are authorized to be appropriated such sums as may be necessary.

42 USC 243 note.

Government
organization.

SEC. 208. FOOD ALLERGIES RESEARCH.

(a) IN GENERAL.—The Secretary of Health and Human Services, acting through the Director of the National Institutes of Health, shall convene an ad hoc panel of nationally recognized experts in allergy and immunology to review current basic and clinical research efforts related to food allergies.

Deadline.
Public
information.

(b) RECOMMENDATIONS.—Not later than 1 year after the date of enactment of this Act, the panel shall make recommendations to the Secretary for enhancing and coordinating research activities concerning food allergies, which the Secretary shall make public.

SEC. 209. FOOD ALLERGENS IN THE FOOD CODE.

The Secretary of Health and Human Services shall, in the Conference for Food Protection, as part of its efforts to encourage cooperative activities between the States under section 311 of the Public Health Service Act (42 U.S.C. 243), pursue revision of the Food Code to provide guidelines for preparing allergen-free foods in food establishments, including in restaurants, grocery store delicatessens and bakeries, and elementary and secondary school cafeterias. The Secretary shall consider guidelines and recommendations developed by public and private entities for public and private food establishments for preparing allergen-free foods in pursuing this revision.

SEC. 210. RECOMMENDATIONS REGARDING RESPONDING TO FOOD-RELATED ALLERGIC RESPONSES.

42 USC 300d–2 note.

The Secretary of Health and Human Services shall, in providing technical assistance relating to trauma care and emergency medical services to State and local agencies under section 1202(b)(3) of the Public Health Service Act (42 U.S.C. 300d–2(b)(3)), include technical assistance relating to the use of different modes of treatment for and prevention of allergic responses to foods.

Approved August 2, 2004.

LEGISLATIVE HISTORY—S. 741:

HOUSE REPORTS: No. 108–608 (Comm. on Energy and Commerce).
SENATE REPORTS: No. 108–226 (Comm. on Health, Education, Labor, and Pensions).
CONGRESSIONAL RECORD, Vol. 150 (2004):
  Mar. 8, considered and passed Senate.
  July 20, considered and passed House.

○

2009 FDA FOOD CODE

2009 FDA FOOD CODE RELEASED NOVEMBER 9, 2009. 2009 FDA Food Code is the seventh full edition of the Food Code Published by the FDA. Full editions of the Food Code are published approximately every four years with supplements published as required between full editions. The last full edition published was 2005 with a supplement published in 2007.

The new FDA Food Code is presented as a model code and reference document that has a sound scientific technical and legal base for the regulation of the retail and food service industries. The code is key to ensure the health and safety of the public through maintaining an overall safe food supply.

The Food Code serves as a national model for "state, city, county, tribal, territorial agencies and industry." The state, city, county, tribal and territorial agencies regulate over 1 million restaurants, retail food stores, and vending and food service operations serving institutions such as schools, hospitals, nursing homes, and child care centers. The model FDA Food Code is the primary contributor to most of these agencies food statutes, regulations and ordinances that govern licensing, inspection, and enforcement requirements.

Agencies contributing to the 2009 FDA Food Code include The Centers for Disease Control and Prevention of the U.S. Department of Health and Human Services and the Food Safety and Inspection Service of the U.S. Department of Agriculture and each was consulted on the changes in the new code with regard to the areas that affect their agencies.

The general purpose of the new 2009 FDA Food Code is "Release of the FDA Food Code provides all levels of government with practical, science-based guidance and manageable, enforceable provisions for mitigating known risks of food borne illness. The FDA Food Code also serves as a reference document for the retail food industry."

"The FDA is spearheading an important initiative to improve the nation's food safety system by establishing a fully integrated national system with federal, state, local, tribal and territorial regulatory agencies," said Dr. Stephen Sundlof, director of FDA's Center for Food Safety and Applied Nutrition. "Food Code adoption and implementation in all jurisdictions are important for achieving uniform national food safety standards and for enhancing the efficiency and effectiveness of our nation's food safety system."

Among several other new additions is "Requirements are added to improve food worker awareness of food allergen concerns in the food service and retail setting." The specific language for these requirements are contained in FDA FOOD CODE 2000: CHAPTER 2-MANAGEMENT AND PERSONNEL, section of the code.

This section of the code provides that the "PERSON IN CHARGE" or designated PERSON IN CHARGE shall be present during all hours of operation and that they shall demonstrate to REGULATORY AUTHORITY knowledge of foodborne disease prevention application of the HAZARD ANALYSIS AND CRITICAL CONTROL POINT principles, and the requirements of this code, which now includes knowledge of food allergies and the appropriate handling of food allergens in order to insure the safety of the public. The PERSON IN CHARGE must be "certified" by passing a test that is part of an accredited program or respond correctly to the inspector's questions as they relate to the specific food operation.

The PERSON IN CHARGE must also ensure that all individuals under their supervision are able to demonstrate the requisite knowledge in food allergy issues as they pertain to their areas of responsibility. The section of the 2009 FDA Food Code that specifically pertains to the new food allergens is included in this manual for a full copy of the code please contact:

U.S. Department of Commerce
Technology Administration
National Technical Information Service
5301 Shawnee Road, Alexandria, VA 22312
(703) 605-6040: TDD: (703) 487-4639
Refer to report number PB2009112613

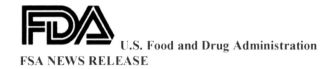

U.S. Food and Drug Administration

FSA NEWS RELEASE

FDA Releases 2013 Food Code: Updated Code is a Model for State, City, County, Tribal, Territorial Agencies and Industry

Center for Food Safety and Applied Nutrition · Food and Drug Administration

November 14, 2013

The U.S. Food and Drug Administration (FDA) issued the 2013 edition of the FDA Food Code on November 13, 2013. Release of this model food code provides all levels of government and industry with practical, science-based guidance and manageable provisions for mitigating known risks of foodborne illness.

The FDA Food Code marks its 20th anniversary with the release of the 2013 edition. The Food Code is a key component of the President's public-health focused framework for maintaining a safe food supply. It represents FDA's best advice for a uniform system of provisions that address the safety and protection of food offered at retail and in food service, and has been widely adopted by state, local, tribal and territorial regulatory agencies that regulate more than one million restaurants, retail food stores, vending operations and food service operations in schools, hospitals, nursing homes, and child care centers.

Significant changes to the 2013 Food Code include the following:

- Restaurants and food stores must post signs notifying their customers that inspection information is available for review.
- Nontyphoidal *Salmonella* is added to the list of illnesses that food workers are required to report to their management and that prompts management to exclude or restrict employees from working with food.
- New requirements that better address emerging trends in food establishments such as the use of reduced oxygen packaging methods and the reuse and refilling of take-home food containers.
- Revisions to the minimum cooking temperatures associated with procedures such as non-continuous cooking and circumstances under which bare-hand contact with ready-to-eat foods is permitted.
- Stronger requirements for cleaning and sanitizing equipment used in preparing raw foods that are major food allergens.

The 2013 edition reflects the input of regulatory officials, industry, academia, and consumers that participated in the 2012 meeting of the Conference for Food Protection (CFP). Collaboration with the CFP and our partners at the U.S. Department of Agriculture's Food Safety and Inspection Service and the Centers for Disease Control and Prevention of the U.S. Department of Health and Human Services helps ensure the Food Code establishes sound requirements that prevent foodborne illness and injury and eliminates the most important food safety hazards in retail and foodservice facilities.

FDA encourages its state, local, tribal, and territorial partners to adopt the latest version of the FDA Food Code. The benefits associated with complete and widespread adoption of the 2013 Food Code as statutes, codes and ordinances include:

- Reduction of the risk of foodborne illnesses within food establishments, thus protecting consumers and industry from potentially devastating health consequences and financial losses.
- Uniform standards for retail food safety that reduce complexity and better ensure compliance.
- The elimination of redundant processes for establishing food safety criteria.
- The establishment of a more standardized approach to inspections and audits of food establishments.

Members of FDA's National Retail Food Team are available to assist regulatory officials, educators, and the industry in their efforts to adopt, implement, and understand the provisions of the FDA Food Code and the Retail Program Standards. Inquiries may be sent to retailfoodprotectionteam@fda.hhs.gov or directly to a Regional Retail Food Specialist located in one of FDA's five Regional Offices across the country.

The 2013 FDA Food Code is available on the FDA website at http://www.fda.gov/FoodCode[1].

Page Last Updated: 11/14/2013

The Food Code is a model for safeguarding public health and ensuring food is unadulterated and honestly presented when offered to the consumer. It represents FDA's best advice for a uniform system of provisions that address the safety and protection of food offered at retail and in food service.

This model is offered for adoption by local, state, and federal governmental jurisdictions for administration by the various departments, agencies, bureaus, divisions, and other units within each jurisdiction that have been delegated compliance responsibilities for food service, retail food stores, or food vending operations. Alternatives that offer an equivalent level of public health protection to ensure that food at retail and foodservice is safe are recognized in this model.

U.S. Department of Commerce National
Technical Information Service
5301 Shawnee Road, Alexandria, VA 22312
Phone: 1-800-553-6847
refer to report number PB2013-110462

ISBN 978-1-935239-02-4

Responsibility

2-101.11 Assignment.

(A) Except as specified in ¶ (B) of this section, the PERMIT HOLDER shall be the PERSON IN CHARGE or shall designate a PERSON IN CHARGE and shall ensure that a PERSON IN CHARGE is present at the FOOD ESTABLISHMENT during all hours of operation.^Pf

(B) In a FOOD ESTABLISHMENT with two or more separately PERMITTED departments that are the legal responsibility of the same PERMIT HOLDER and that are located on the same PREMISES, the PERMIT HOLDER may, during specific time periods when food is not being prepared, packaged, or served, designate a single PERSON IN CHARGE who is present on the PREMISES during all hours of operation, and who is responsible for each separately PERMITTED FOOD ESTABLISHMENT on the PREMISES.^Pf

Knowledge

2-102.11 Demonstration.

Based on the RISKS inherent to the FOOD operation, during inspections and upon request the PERSON IN CHARGE shall demonstrate to the REGULATORY AUTHORITY knowledge of foodborne disease prevention, application of the HAZARD Analysis and CRITICAL CONTROL POINT principles, and the requirements of this Code. The PERSON IN CHARGE shall demonstrate this knowledge by:

(A) Complying with this Code by having no violations of PRIORITY ITEMS during the current inspection;^Pf

(B) Being a certified FOOD protection manager who has shown proficiency of required information through passing a test that is part of an ACCREDITED PROGRAM;^Pf or

(C) Responding correctly to the inspector's questions as they relate to the specific FOOD operation. The areas of knowledge include:

(1) Describing the relationship between the prevention of foodborne disease and the personal hygiene of a FOOD EMPLOYEE;^Pf

(2) Explaining the responsibility of the PERSON IN CHARGE for preventing the transmission of foodborne disease by a FOOD EMPLOYEE who has a disease or medical condition that may cause foodborne disease;^Pf

(3) Describing the symptoms associated with the diseases that are transmissible through FOOD;^Pf

(4) Explaining the significance of the relationship between maintaining the time and temperature of TIME/TEMPERATURE CONTROL FOR SAFETY FOOD and the prevention of foodborne illness;^Pf

(5) Explaining the HAZARDS involved in the consumption of raw or undercooked MEAT, POULTRY, EGGS, and FISH;^Pf

(6) Stating the required FOOD temperatures and times for safe cooking of TIME/TEMPERATURE CONTROL FOR SAFETY FOOD including MEAT, POULTRY, EGGS, and FISH;^Pf

(7) Stating the required temperatures and times for the safe refrigerated storage, hot holding, cooling, and reheating of TIME/TEMPERATURE CONTROL FOR SAFETY FOOD;^Pf

(8) Describing the relationship between the prevention of foodborne illness and the management and control of the following:
(a) Cross contamination,^Pf
(b) Hand contact with READY-TO-EAT FOODS,^Pf
(c) Handwashing,^Pf and
(d) Maintaining the FOOD ESTABLISHMENT in a clean condition and in good repair;^Pf

(9) Describing FOODS identified as MAJOR FOOD ALLERGENS and the symptoms that a MAJOR FOOD ALLERGEN could cause in a sensitive individual who has an allergic reaction.^Pf

(10) Explaining the relationship between FOOD safety and providing EQUIPMENT that is:
(a) Sufficient in number and capacity,^Pf and
(b) Properly designed, constructed, located, installed, operated, maintained, and cleaned;^Pf

(11) Explaining correct procedures for cleaning and SANITIZING UTENSILS and FOOD-CONTACT SURFACES of EQUIPMENT;[Pf]

(12) Identifying the source of water used and measures taken to ensure that it remains protected from contamination such as providing protection from backflow and precluding the creation of cross connections;[Pf]

(13) Identifying POISONOUS OR TOXIC MATERIALS in the FOOD ESTABLISHMENT and the procedures necessary to ensure that they are safely stored, dispensed, used, and disposed of according to LAW;[Pf]

(14) Identifying CRITICAL CONTROL POINTS in the operation from purchasing through sale or service that when not controlled may contribute to the transmission of foodborne illness and explaining steps taken to ensure that the points are controlled in accordance with the requirements of this Code;[Pf]

(15) Explaining the details of how the PERSON IN CHARGE and FOOD EMPLOYEES comply with the HACCP PLAN if a plan is required by the LAW, this Code, or an agreement between the REGULATORY AUTHORITY and the FOOD ESTABLISHMENT;[Pf]

(16) Explaining the responsibilities, rights, and authorities assigned by this Code to the:
(a) FOOD EMPLOYEE,[Pf]
(b) CONDITIONAL EMPLOYEE,[Pf]
(c) PERSON IN CHARGE,[Pf]
(d) REGULATORY AUTHORITY;[Pf] and

(17) Explaining how the PERSON IN CHARGE, FOOD EMPLOYEES, and FOOD EMPLOYEESS comply with reporting responsibilities and EXCLUSION or RESTRICTION of FOOD EMPLOYEES.[Pf]

2-102.12 Certified Food Protection Manager

(A) At least one EMPLOYEES that has supervisory and management responsibility and the authority to direct and control FOOD preparation and service shall be a certified FOOD protection manager who has shown proficiency of required

information through passing a test that is part of an ACCREDITED PROGRAM.

(B) *This section does not apply to certain types of FOOD ESTABLISHMENTS deemed by the REGULATORY AUTHORITY to pose minimal risk of causing, or contributing to, foodborne illness based on the nature of the operation and extent of FOOD preparation.*

2-102.20 Food Protection Manager Certification.

(A) A PERSON IN CHARGE who demonstrates knowledge by being a FOOD protection manager that is certified by a FOOD protection manager certification program that is evaluated and listed by a Conference for Food Protection-recognized accrediting agency as conforming to the Conference for Food Protection Standards for Accreditation of FOOD Protection Manager Certification Programs is deemed to comply with ¶2-102.11(B).

(B) A FOOD ESTABLISHMENT that has an EMPLOYEES that is certified by a FOOD protection manager certification program that is evaluated and listed by a Conference for Food Protection-recognized accrediting agency as conforming to the Conference for Food Protection Standards for Accreditation of FOOD Protection Manager Certification Programs is deemed to comply with §2-102.12.

Duties 2-103.11 Person in Charge.

The PERSON IN CHARGE shall ensure that:

(A) FOOD ESTABLISHMENT operations are not conducted in a private home or in a room used as living or sleeping quarters as specified under § 6-202.111;[Pf]

(B) PERSONS unnecessary to the FOOD ESTABLISHMENT operation are not allowed in the FOOD preparation, FOOD storage, or WAREWASHING areas, except that brief visits and tours may be authorized by the PERSON IN CHARGE if steps are taken to ensure that exposed FOOD; clean EQUIPMENT, UTENSILS, and LINENS; and unwrapped SINGLE-SERVICE and SINGLE-USE ARTICLES are protected from contamination;[Pf]

(C) EMPLOYEES and other PERSONS such as delivery and maintenance PERSONS and pesticide applicators entering the FOOD preparation, FOOD storage, and WAREWASHING areas comply with this Code;[Pf]

(D) EMPLOYEES are effectively cleaning their hands, by routinely monitoring the EMPLOYEES' handwashing;[Pf]

(E) EMPLOYEES are visibly observing FOODS as they are received to determine that they are from APPROVED sources, delivered at the required temperatures, protected from contamination, UNADULTERED, and accurately presented, by routinely monitoring the EMPLOYEES' observations and periodically evaluating FOODS upon their receipt;[Pf]

(F) EMPLOYEES are verifying that FOODS delivered to the FOOD ESTABLISHMENT during non-operating hours are from APPROVED sources and are placed into appropriate storage locations such that they are maintained at the required temperatures, protected from contamination, UNADULTERED, and accurately presented;[Pf]

(G) EMPLOYEES are properly cooking TIME/TEMPERATURE CONTROL FOR SAFETY FOOD, being particularly careful in cooking those FOODS known to cause severe foodborne illness and death, such as EGGS and COMMINUTED MEATS, through daily oversight of the EMPLOYEES' routine monitoring of the cooking temperatures using appropriate temperature measuring devices properly scaled and calibrated as specified under § 4-203.11 and ¶ 4-502.11(B);[Pf]

(H) EMPLOYEES are using proper methods to rapidly cool TIME/TEMPERATURE CONTROL FOR SAFETY FOOD that are not held hot or are not for consumption within 4 hours, through daily oversight of the EMPLOYEES' routine monitoring of FOOD temperatures during cooling;[Pf]

(I) CONSUMERS who order raw; or partially cooked READY-TO-EAT FOODS of animal origin are informed as specified under § 3-603.11 that the FOOD is not cooked sufficiently to ensure its safety;[Pf]

(J) EMPLOYEES are properly SANITIZING cleaned multiuse EQUIPMENT and UTENSILS before they are reused, through routine monitoring of solution temperature and exposure time for hot water SANITIZING, and chemical concentration, pH, temperature, and exposure time for chemical SANITIZING;[Pf]

(K) CONSUMERS are notified that clean TABLEWARE is to be used when they return to self-service areas such as salad bars and buffets as specified under § 3-304.16;[Pf]

(L) Except when APPROVAL is obtained from the REGULATORY AUTHORITY as specified in ¶ 3-301.11(E), EMPLOYEES are preventing cross-contamination of READY-TO-EAT FOOD with bare hands by properly using suitable UTENSILS such as deli tissue, spatulas, tongs, single-use gloves, or dispensing EQUIPMENT;[Pf]

(M) EMPLOYEES are properly trained in FOOD safety, including FOOD allergy awareness, as it relates to their assigned duties;[Pf]

(N) FOOD EMPLOYEES and CONDITIONAL EMPLOYEES are informed in a verifiable manner of their responsibility to report in accordance with LAW, to the PERSON IN CHARGE, information about their health and activities as they relate to diseases that are transmissible through FOOD, as specified under ¶ 2-201.11(A);[Pf] and

(O) Written procedures and plans, where specified by this Code and as developed by the FOOD ESTABLISHMENT, are maintained and implemented as required.[Pf]

— — — — — — — — — —

The yellow highlights on pages 20 and 21 were added by SpotCheck as highlights.

The use of italics, small caps, and the "pf" superscript is verbatim from the 2013 Food Code, they are explained in Section 8 of the Preface of the Food Code, *Information to Assist the User.* Here is the link to the Code:

http://www.fda.gov/downloads/Food/GuidanceRegulation/retailfoodprotection/foodcode/UCM374510.pdf

The Food and Drug Administration (FDA) and the Centers for Disease Control and Prevention (CDC) of the U.S. Department of Health and Human Services (HHS) and the Food Safety and Inspection Service of the U.S. Department of Agriculture (USDA) are pleased to announce the release of the 2013 and eighth edition of the Food Code. The Food Code is a model code and reference document for state, city, county and tribal agencies that regulate operations such as restaurants, retail food stores, food vendors, and foodservice operations in institutions such as schools, hospitals, assisted living, nursing homes and child care centers. Food safety practices at these facilities play a critical role in preventing foodborne illness. The Food Code establishes practical, science-based guidance for mitigating risk factors that are known to cause or contribute to foodborne illness outbreaks associated with retail and foodservice establishments and is an important part of strengthening our nation's food protection system.

As of 2012, all 50 states and 3 of 6 territories report having retail codes patterned after previous editions of the Food Code. We strongly encourage the adoption and implementation of the 2013 Food Code at all levels of government.

This edition of the Food Code reflects our current understanding of evidenced-based practices for the effective control of microbiological, chemical and physical hazards in food facilities that can cause foodborne illness. Many of the changes to this edition reflect recommendations made at the 2012 biennial meeting of the Conference for Food Protection, a national organization that affords scientists and policy makers from all levels of government, industry, academia and consumers the opportunity to propose and deliberate on improvements to the Food Code.

The federal government is committed to enhanced coordination with state, local, and tribal agencies, and the food industry to protect our food supply, and the Food Code is one important element in this strategy. HHS and USDA will continue to take progressive steps to partner with all who have a stake in food safety, and are committed to reducing the incidence of foodborne illness in the United States.

Margaret A. Hamburg, M.D.
Commissioner
Food and Drug Administration
U.S. Department of Health and Human Services

Alfred V. Almanza
Administrator
Food Safety and Inspection Service
U.S. Department of Agriculture

Thomas R. Frieden, M.D., M.P.H
Director
Centers for Disease Control and Prevention
U.S. Department of Health and Human Services

ONTARIO LEGISLATIVE ASSEMBLY BILL 3
Sabrina's Law, 2005, S.O., c. 7

Ontario Legislative Assembly Bill 3, May 16, 2005. Known as Sabrina's Law, 2005, S.O., c. 7, passed by Ontario's Legislative Assembly on May 16, 2005.

This law, which was the first of its kind in Canada, requires Ontario school boards to have policies to deal with students at risk of anaphylaxis.

The law which became mandatory January 1, 2006, is named in memory of Sabrina Shannon.

Sabrina Shannon was a bright, happy 13-year-old 8th grader with food allergies. On September 29, 2003, Sabrina was at the end of her first month of the new school year and eager to join her classmates in the enjoyment of the school cafeteria's food. Sabrina was extremely cautious about her food allergies and always demonstrated excellent judgment in her food selections. Just the previous week she enjoyed the French fries after first checking that they did not contain any of her allergens.

Sara Shannon, Sabrina's mom, knew how diligent her daughter was with regard to her allergies capitulated, and instead of Sabrina's usual allergy-free packed lunch allowed her to take $5.00 for a school lunch. Sabrina left her home that morning with her EpiPen and her asthma puffer in her backpack looking forward to another day at school with her friends.

Just before noon, Sabrina and her best friend headed off to the cafeteria for lunch. After making sure again that the fries were free of her allergens, she ordered them and sat down to eat. In her class immediately following lunch Sabrina began to wheeze. Attributing her breathing difficulties to her asthma, Sabrina went straight to the school office located at the opposite end of the building. By the time Sabrina arrived she was experiencing advancing respiratory distress, and kept telling office staff "it's my asthma." Just in case this was a food allergy reaction, a teacher rushed to Sabrina's locker to retrieve her EpiPen while school officials summoned an ambulance. Tragically, before the EpiPen could be administered and prior to the arrival of the ambulance, Sabrina collapsed, lost consciousness and went into cardiac arrest.

Sabrina was transported to the local hospital and after her heart was restarted and she was stabilized, she was airlifted to Children's Hospital of Eastern Ontario in Ottawa. Despite all efforts by medical staff it was impossible to restore functioning to Sabrina's oxygen-starved brain. On September 30, 2003 just one day after her reaction the agonizing decision was made to remove her from life support and Sabrina died.

Subsequent investigation into the incident revealed that her catastrophic medical condition had been caused by an anaphylactic reaction to food. Despite Sabrina's inquiries into the food preparation she could not know that her lunch selection would be served using tongs that had served a food to which she was allergic. The simple act of using the same utensil to serve multiple foods had cost the life of the much beloved teenager.

Sara Shannon made a promise to her daughter that she would do all she could to prevent this from happening to any other child. Through her efforts and the efforts of others, she kept her promise with the passage of this law. At the time, this law was the most progressive in Canada and the U.S. Since its passage, Alberta, British Columbia, Manitoba, New Brunswick, Nova Scotia, Prince Edward Island and the U.S. have all made changes in public policies, laws and guidelines to ensure the safety of children and adults with regard to food allergens.

Canada is currently considering national enhanced labeling for food allergens, gluten sources and added sulphites as proposed in the regulatory project 1220. As of the date of this printing these changes are under review and officials are responding to comments.

WHAT IS A FOOD ALLERGY?

WHAT IS A FOOD ALLERGY?

What Is a Food Allergy

Food allergies have long been debated in the medical and scientific communities. For the purposes of our program we will use the most broadly accepted definition.

Food Allergy: The body's physiological response to a food it sees as harmful. When the body encounters these foods it triggers an immune system reaction to fight the invader. Once the immune system deems a food as harmful it creates antibodies to deal with it. The antibody that plays a major role in allergic food reactions is Immunoglobulin E (IgE).

The next time the body encounters the offending food it floods the system with massive amount of chemicals to combat the invader. Unfortunately, the chemicals trigger a multitude of allergic symptoms, some of which are violent and can be fatal.

Food Allergy Reactions:

Food allergy reactions and symptoms can be quite diverse. They may affect one or several organs all at once. Reactions range from mild to severe to life-threatening. They usually appear within one to fifteen minutes but may develop over a period of hours after contact with the offending food.

Milder food allergy reaction symptoms may be as subtle as hoarseness, hiccups, fullness in the ears, throat tightness, redness of the skin, itchiness or mild swelling at the points of contact.

The most severe of the body's reactions is known as anaphylaxis. For our purposes we will use the simple definition of anaphylaxis.

Anaphylaxis: A serious allergic reaction that is usually rapid in onset and may cause death.

> *The general symptoms of anaphylaxis are: itching in and around the mouth, tightening of the throat causing airway blockage, wheezing, hoarseness, shortness of breath, red welts or hives, swelling of eyelids, lips, hands or feet, nausea, cramping, vomiting, confusion, sense of impending doom, drop in blood pressure, loss of consciousness.*

> *At its severest, an anaphylactic reaction will affect the cardiovascular and respiratory systems, and along with low blood pressure will cause shock, collapse, and if untreated, death.*

> *Over one million individuals are hospitalized each year due to anaphylactic reactions.*

Food Intolerances and Sensitivities:

Food intolerances and sensitivities: Any negative physical reaction to a food or foods.

WHAT IS A FOOD ALLERGY?

Food intolerance and sensitivity symptoms such as allergies are varied and range from mild to severe. Symptoms include:

- headaches, migraines,
- fatigue,
- depression/anxiety, hyperactivity (children),
- mouth ulcers, stomach ulcers, duodenal ulcers,
- aching muscles,
- vomiting and nausea,
- diarrhea, irritable bowel syndrome, constipation, gas, bloating onset Crohn's disease,
- joint pain, rheumatoid arthritis, and
- water retention, rashes and hives.

The three major diseases associated with food allergy intolerances and sensitivities are asthma, eczema, and allergenic rhinitis or hay fever.

Celiac disease: One disease specific to food is celiac disease. In this disease there is one culprit, gluten. Gluten is a complex group of proteins found in wheat, barley and rye. Symptoms include: diarrhea, abdominal pain, bloating, weight loss, malaise, weakness, irritability, and recurrent mouth ulcers.

Celiac disease causes irreversible damage to the intestine. The disease is degenerative, with each exposure to gluten causing further damage. The damage prevents the body from absorbing nutrients while at the same time causing the leakage of large molecules through the intestinal wall that normally are not able to penetrate the intestinal wall. In addition to causing severe pain, celiac disease will frequently leave sufferers malnourished.

The Cure

There is no known cure for food allergies, food intolerances, food sensitivities or celiac disease. The only effective treatment strategy is strict — no contact with the food.

Some individuals may be so sensitive that even touching residue or breathing vapor may cause a severe reaction. Reactions can start within a minute and last from hours to days. Many who suffer from anaphylaxis require more than one course of treatment, one immediately and one or more several hours later. Victims frequently are under medical supervision for 12 hours or more. Others will suffer for days after the event and for some there will be permanent physical damage and even death. Experts estimate that the financial impact to society from hospital and medical bills and loss of income is in the billions! There is of course no measure possible for the physical and emotional toll.

WHAT IS A FOOD ALLERGY?

How Many People Seek Medical Aid Annually?

The CDC reports that annually over 50,000 people seek emergency aid for food-related allergic reactions and that over 200 will die. It is estimated that over 125,000 more will seek medical help from clinics and private practice physicians. Medical professionals interviewed state these incidents are "grossly under reported" and that these numbers should be far higher. We know that there are over 2,500 emergency facilities in the U.S. and in five of these facilities alone they saw hundreds of cases. We have no idea how many self treat.

How Many People are Affected by Food Allergies?

According to the CDC, medical professionals and the scientific community, from 2½ to 4% of Americans suffer from food allergies; in Canada the numbers are 1 to 2% of adults and 3 to 8% of children.

How Many People are Affected by Food Intolerances or Sensitivities?

According to medical professionals and the scientific community, between 10 to 25% of Americans, 10 to 30% of Canadians and 30 to 50% of England's population suffer from food intolerances or sensitivities.

With the current U.S. population at 303,824,650 as reported in the 2008 Census, the estimated numbers of individuals affected are from 45,573,698 at the low end to 88,109,148 at the high end. Current estimates by the scientific community tell us that between 2.5 and 4% of the U.S. population have food allergies and an additional 10 to 25% suffer from food intolerances and food sensitivities. Estimates in Canada reflect that 2% of adult population and between 3 and 8% of children suffer from food allergies, with the incidences of food intolerances and sensitivities ranging from 10 to 30% of the population. Based on the Canada statistics from March 2010, population numbers of 34,060,000 equates to a minimum of 4,087,200 and a maximum of 10,218,000 individuals who have some sort of negative physical reaction to one or more foods.

The estimates for England are even higher with 30 to 50% of the population suffering from food allergies, intolerances or sensitivities. The Office for National Statistics 2008 national population projections of 51,460,000 equate to between 15,438,000 and 25,730,000 individuals who have some sort of negative physical reaction to one or more foods.

Many of these individuals will react to more than one food. All affected individuals interviewed reported that food allergies, food intolerances and food sensitivities impacted their daily lives, some profoundly. Their food issues directly influenced:
- Where they ate
- Where they shopped
- What events they attended
- Where they vacationed
- Where they stayed

WHAT IS A FOOD ALLERGY?

- What school or day care they used
- What form of transportation they utilized

Without exception all agree that when they identify a restaurant, deli, store, bakery, lodging facility or transportation carrier that they and their families, friends and business associates know can handle and will accommodate their food issue, these facilities become their establishments of choice. Many reported these businesses receive their patronage exclusively.

What Are the Most Common Food Allergies?

90% of food reactions are caused by eight foods. These major food allergens are referred to as the Big 8 Allergens in the U.S.; Canada also recognizes Sesame as a major allergen.

The Major Allergens:

• Milk	• Tree Nuts	• Wheat
• Eggs	• Fish	• Soy
• Peanuts	• Shell Fish	• Sesame

The Big 8 Allergens are the focus of the Food Labeling and Consumer Protection Act. Canada adds Sesame to the list. These nine are the main focus of our training. The Big 8 are the eight allergens required by U.S. law and enforced by the FDA that must be identified in plain language on food labels. While this is a requirement, the Big 8 Allergens and Sesame may appear under many names and may hide in places we would not think to look.

Other Names and Hidden Sources of the Big 8 Allergens and Sesame:

Other Names for Milk	Common Hidden Sources of Milk
Artificial butter oil	Yogurt
Buttermilk	Butter
Caramel	Margarine
Casein, Caseinate	Cheese curds
Cheese cream curds	Creams
Whey, dried milk	Custards, puddings, semolina, tapioca, sago
High-protein flavin	Hot dogs, meatballs
Lactoglobulin	Spam
Lactalbumin	Frozen desserts
Lactose	Pizza
Natural flavoring	Coffee creamers including non-dairy
Rennet	Asian fruit beverages & canned tuna
	Sauces, béchamel, parsley, hollandaise, etc.
	Many packaged foods & soups
	Pastries, rolls, cakes, cookies, scones, white bread

While this list is reasonably comprehensive it cannot include all items, be sure to read labels carefully.

WHAT IS A FOOD ALLERGY?

Other Names for Eggs	Common Hidden Sources of Eggs
Albumin	Bagels, pretzels
Binder	Baked goods
Coagulant	Bouillon
Egg White	Cereals, cakes, chocolate, custards, meringues
Egg Yolk	Commercial pasta
Emulsifier	Cream sauces, canned soups
Globulin	Coffee drinks
Lecithin	Battered meats & fish, some margarines
Levetin	French toast, pancakes, waffles, batters
Lysozyme	Ice creams, sherbets, frozen desserts
Ovovitellin	Instant mashed potatoes
Ovalbumin	Tartar sauce
Ovomucoid	White batter-fried foods, wines cleared with egg
Powdered egg	Mayonnaise, marshmallows
Vitellin	Pasta, pies, puddings
Whole egg albumin	Processed meats
	Marzipan

* While this list is reasonably comprehensive it cannot include all items, be sure to read labels carefully.

Other Names for Peanuts	Common Hidden Sources of Peanuts
Artificial nuts	Cakes, pastries, cookies, crackers
Imitation nuts	Biscuits
Beer nuts	Ice creams
Goober peas	Desserts & dessert toppings
Emulsifiers	Confectionery and savory snacks
Nut spreads	Breakfast cereals
Praline	Meat products
Marzipan	Vegetarian products
Frangipani	Ready-made meals
Hydrolyzed vegetable protein	Amaretto products, macaroons
	Worcestershire, satay & curry sauces
	Chili, molé

While this list is reasonably comprehensive it cannot include all items, be sure to read labels carefully.

WHAT IS A FOOD ALLERGY?

Names for Tree Nuts

Almonds
Brazil nuts
Cashews
Hazelnuts/Filberts
Pecans
Pine nuts
Pistachios
Chestnuts & acorns
Macadamia nuts
Tiger nuts (earth almonds)
Walnuts
Coconut & nutmeg *(rare reactions)*

Common Hidden Sources of Tree Nuts

Candies, cookies, cereals, desserts
Donuts, sauces, pesto sauces, stuffing mixes
Popcorn, nougat, praline, marzipan
Cheese spreads, chocolates, ice creams
Worcestershire sauces, gluten-free breads
Granola bars, vegetarian foods, pastries & artificial nuts
Amaretto liquors, coffee flavorings

* While this list is reasonably comprehensive it cannot include all items, be sure to read labels carefully.

Names for Seafood (fish and shellfish)

Bony Finfish	Crustaceans	Mollusks
Cod	Lobster	Abalone
Hake	Shrimp	Snail
Halibut	Crab	Limpet
Sardine	Crayfish	Squid
Mackerel	Rock lobster	Clam
Snapper	Langoustine	Mussel
Tilapia		Oyster
Tuna		Scallop
Ray		
Shark		
Salmon		

Hidden Sources of Seafood

Anchovy
Capone and Sicilian relish
Caviar
Imitation crab/crab legs
Pizza toppings
Fish skin used in fining

Caesar salad
Worcestershire and marinara sauces
Surimi & Alaskan Pollock
Hot dogs
Bologna, lunch meats & ham
Soups, stocks & sauces

While this list is reasonably comprehensive it cannot include all items, be sure to read labels carefully.

WHAT IS A FOOD ALLERGY?

Other Names for Wheat/Gluten

Cereal binders, fillers, protein, starch
Hydrolyzed plant/vegetable proteins
Bran
Bulgur (cracked wheat) flour
Farina
Gluten
Modified starch proteins
Modified vegetable proteins
Semolina
All flours
Caramel
Citric acid (non U.S. made)
Dextrin
Diglycerides (may contain gluten)
Starch edible, food (may say modified)
Gum base (may contain gluten)
Malt/malt flavoring (may contain gluten)
Maltodextrim (non U.S. made)
Monoglycerides (may contain gluten)
MSG (may contain gluten)
Natural flavorings (may contain wheat
  or milk)
Vegetable protein, gum, starch
Textured vegetable protein

Common Hidden Sources of Wheat/Gluten

Bread, pita, nan, pizza, poppadoms
Baked goods, chapattis
Pastries
Pasta
Cereals, crackers
Processed meats, spices
Cakes, cookies
Snack foods
Polish wheat or Kamut
Flours: bread, brown, graham,
  hard, strong, whole meal, ganary,
  bulgur wheat, bran, chilton, dinkel,
  couscous, durum, einkorn, faro,
  fu, germ, spelt, triticum, triticale
Udon noodles, sauces, gravies
Soups, many mueslis, candies
Blue cheese, cottage cheese
Cream cheese, ground spices
Mustard powder, stock cubes
Rice milk, some soy milk, soy sauce
Miso, ice cream, salad dressings
Icing sugar (depending on country)
Whiskey, gin, white vinegar, French fries
Beer

* While this list is reasonably comprehensive it cannot include all items, be sure to read labels carefully.

Other Names for Soy

Lecithin
Vegetable gum
Vegetable protein
Textured vegetable protein
Vegetable starch

Common Hidden Sources of Soy

Cereals, crackers, soups, baked goods
Sauces, soups, canned tuna, tamari
Vegetarian burgers, risottos, sausage rolls
Meatballs, kebab, soy sauce, miso, snacks
Many gluten-free breads & products
Deli meats, hot dogs, vegan products
Vegetable/non-stick spray
Chocolate, flavored teas

While this list is reasonably comprehensive it cannot include all items, be sure to read labels carefully.

Other Names for Sesame	Common Hidden Sources of Sesame
Benne	Halva, teheni, tahini, tahina, rolls, burger buns, breads
Teel or Till	Bagels, bread sticks, crackers, snack bars
Simsim	Snacks, veggie burgers, rice cakes, cookies
Anjoli	Salad dressings, humus, stir fries, Asian foods
Cingili	Mixed spices, processed meats, sausages, sauces
	Chutneys, cakes, beverages

While this list is reasonably comprehensive it cannot include all items, be sure to read labels carefully.

The major components that cause most food reactions are the proteins in these foods. It is important to remember that proteins *are not killed or eliminated by rinsing, wiping or heat,* **you must wash, sanitize and remove all residue.**

Additionally, proteins can be transmitted in vapor, steam and residue.

Food Allergy Safe
Case Studies

Big 8 Allergen

Milk

Food Allergy Safe
CASE STUDY: JASON

Background

Jason is an active five year old with a talent for getting into everything. Jason has been allergic to cow's milk from infancy. His first reaction resulted in severe vomiting and diarrhea. Jason ended up in the hospital severely dehydrated. After a few days stay in the hospital Mom and Dad took him home. After the second episode Jason's allergy was detected and all cow's milk was eliminated from his diet.

Event

One day five-year-old Jason went out to eat with his family. Mom and Dad, as was their habit, informed restaurant personnel of Jason's food allergy. As usual, Jason was his rambunctious self and could not resist diving into the booth where he ended up rolling onto the carpeted floor. A short time later Mom noticed a red patch on his face. Assuming he just irritated his face during his booth dive, she thought little of it. The meal was ordered and Jason wasted no time digging in. The family involved in their food and conversation did not notice the patch on Jason's face spreading. Shortly after gobbling down his meal Jason complained of an upset stomach; it was then they noticed the spreading blotch on his face. Concerned, the family took Jason to the hospital.

On the way to the emergency room Jason began to vomit and was noticeably having trouble breathing. By the time they arrived Jason was barely breathing. He was rushed into the emergency room and immediately received aggressive treatment for his reaction. Jason spent several days in the hospital due to the severity of his reaction.

The parents racked their brains in an attempt to determine the source of his reaction. Their physician was sure it had to have come from the restaurant because of the timeline in the appearance of the red blotches on his face. What was odd is that the red blotch was noticed before any food or drink had been ordered, let alone delivered to the table.

Going back to the restaurant Mom met with the manager and server where they reviewed everything served to the family, and nothing had milk or milk byproducts. None of them could figure out where the five year old came in contact with milk.

While the three of them attempted to solve the riddle the bus person walked by and asked, "What was up?" After hearing the story the bus person asked where they were sitting. Upon learning of their location he asked if Jason was on the floor under the table. Mom recalled the booth dive had indeed resulted in contact with the floor, but other than the red spot on his face, Jason was not hurt. Mom said she corrected his behavior and they went on with their meals.

Food Allergy Safe
CASE STUDY: JASON

It was the bus person who connected the dots. The previous family at the table had spilled a glass of milk and it went everywhere. Even though the table and booth bench were wiped down Jason came in contact with the substance either on the seat, on the carpet or under the table. Regardless, it was enough to trigger his dangerous reaction.

The Consequence:

Because of a spill that was not thoroughly cleaned up a little boy nearly lost his life. Jason was dangerously ill and was mentally and physically traumatized by the experience. The hospital stay was frightening for the child and extremely hard on his parents. Hospital costs were in the thousands and income due to lost work days didn't help. The restaurant's liability was high since they were made aware of Jason's condition prior to seating him. None of the restaurant's employees wanted to injure any one, let alone a little boy. Worst of all the employees wondered how many other people had been injured or exposed to potential injury by just this same kind of oversight.

Big 8 Allergen

Eggs

Food Allergy Safe
CASE STUDY: JOHN

Background

John has been allergic to eggs from early childhood. His first reaction was mild with a light rash as the only indication there was any issue. The second time he ingested eggs however there was a full-blown anaphylactic reaction nearly costing him his life. From that time on John had to have immediate access to an EpiPen.

Growing up, John's parents struggled to keep him away from what seemed to be the ever present ingredient in so many foods: the egg. School was particularly difficult with birthday parties, holiday parties, camp and the school cafeteria. John was even denied access to a science camp because of his allergy; they simply did not want to take the responsibility for his safety. Away from home activities were equally restricted because of his food allergy. John felt left out and many times isolated because of his allergy to eggs.

Even with careful planning and scrutiny, John many times had to use his EpiPen because of eggs or egg byproducts not listed on labels. His parents spent tens of thousands of dollars in hospital bills and several times he had to be transported by emergency vehicles.

As an adult John is very vocal about his allergy. He informs restaurants when making a reservation and upon his arrival makes sure they are very aware of his egg allergy. He insists that his table, chairs, booth seats and backs and all items on the table are well cleaned before he is seated. He further asks to speak to the manager on duty and always emphasizes his condition to the wait staff.

Event

One morning on a business trip, John ordered his breakfast of oatmeal, fresh fruit and a scone. He was careful to inquire about the scone which he knew is not traditionally made with egg. The wait person checked with the kitchen staff and sure enough there was no egg in the scone. The wait person returned to the table and informed John that there was no egg in the scone and the order was placed.

John ate his oatmeal and finished his fresh fruit with the scone. Within minutes of the first few bites of the scone, John was in trouble. He felt flushed and dizzy and was having difficulty breathing. His stomach was churning and he had lower abdominal cramps. John knew he had very little time to employ his EpiPen. John injected himself with the EpiPen and managed to flag down an employee who called for an aid car.

John was transported to the emergency room of the local hospital where two more shots of epinephrine were administered over the next 24 hours. Finally, after a day in critical care observation, John returned to the hotel. After a period of rest John asked to speak to the general manager of the facility. The general manager assured John "he would get to the bottom of the situation."

The next day John again met with the general manager who informed him that while there was no egg in the scone it was covered in an egg substitute wash to help the raw sugar adhere to the top of the scone. John conveyed his confusion to the general manager since he clearly had informed the hostess, restaurant manager, wait person and chef of his allergy.

As it turned out, his wait person thought that egg substitute did not contain egg or egg by-product. Of course this was wrong, almost dead wrong. Further, since the wait person did not put an allergy alert on the order, the busy kitchen had no way of knowing that the order they were preparing was going to a person with an egg allergy. The restaurant manager, busy with the breakfast rush never checked the order. The general manager was horrified that his wait person, who was not new to the establishment or to the business, did not know that egg substitute contained egg.

The Consequence:

John personally was lucky, his EpiPen was close at hand and fortunately he reacted quickly. He was transported upon his request to the hospital. This turned out to be fortunate since John's EpiPen was only a double dose and it took three doses of Epinephrine to combat this reaction. If John had simply returned to his room it is likely he would have died. This very real possibility coupled with the truly frightening physical symptoms of anaphylaxis made for a horrible few days.

Professionally, John missed his business meetings and they could not be rescheduled on this trip. He lost time and suffered business delays which impacted his finances.

The hotel paid for John's medical expenses, his flight and hotel expenses and all out of pocket expenses for his trip. This amounted to over $8,000.00; they further paid for his hotel expenses for his rescheduled business meetings some six weeks later. Fortunately, John did not seek any other financial remuneration from the hotel. Of course the hotel had to deal with the disruption of one of their guests being removed via aid car during the breakfast rush. They further had to deal with the very real possibility that given the wait persons mishandling of the situation and the restaurant manager's lack of attention, there was a very real possibility this could happen again. The next time the guest may not be so lucky!

Big 8 Allergen

Peanuts

Food Allergy Safe
CASE STUDY: DAVID

Background

David, like many allergic to peanuts and peanut products, presented allergic reaction indicators early in life. After a couple of very close calls as a child, David learned not to eat anything his parents didn't prepare or approve. Armed with a double-dose EpiPen at all times, David made the best of his condition.

As a teenager David had a close call at a ball game where he and his parents discovered that either through contact cross contamination or dust-off of peanut shells at the sports stadium, a severe allergic reaction occurred. With quick response by those around him and an immediate injection with his EpiPen David managed to make it to the hospital. During transport by ambulance David required the second dose from his EpiPen. After two days of observation and two more Epinephrine shots David returned home. David visited his physician for a follow-up and was told then he would have to avoid sports stadiums or any other venue where peanut dust might be present.

Event

At 18 David was excited about the 50th wedding anniversary party for his grandparents. The affair was to be held at a lovely property and catered by a well known and highly experienced restaurant chain. The size of the party required the restaurant to use one of the facilities they routinely contracted for just these types of occasions. The restaurant was made aware of the severe peanut allergy of one of the guests and designed a menu with no peanut products. The chef was careful to personally check all ingredients for the appetizers, soup, salad, main course and desserts, ensuring all were peanut-product free.

The party began with a social hour where appetizers were served and after a few speeches and dedications toasted with sparkling cider, the group was seated for dinner. David's first course of lobster bisque was served and as a favorite of his, he as his mother remarked "inhaled it." As the soup bowls were being cleared preparing for the next course David suddenly collapsed. His parents immediately injected him with one of the EpiPens and paramedics were summoned. To his parents' great distress the first injection did not seem to be working and the second injection was administered. To the relief of everyone the second shot seemed to bring him around and David was transported to the hospital.

During transport to the hospital David again began to fail. Upon arrival he was in full cardiac arrest. David was in one of the nation's top-rated trauma centers and despite their best efforts he did not survive.

Food Allergy Safe
CASE STUDY: DAVID

Health officials were called to investigate the incident and an autopsy was ordered. The investigation revealed that the restaurant had indeed noted David's peanut allergy and the menu ingredients selected were peanut and peanut-product free. Investigators knew that peanut allergic reactions occur quickly after exposure to the allergen. This meant the peanut had to be somewhere around or in the appetizers or soup. With the time that elapsed between the appetizers and the soup, the chief suspect quickly became the soup. Had it been environmental, David should have reacted much sooner, so again soup seemed to be the culprit.

The chef was questioned at length and he gave the names of all of the prep cooks involved in the food preparation. The kitchen, prep kitchen and all storage areas were thoroughly inspected. In the prep kitchen next to the stock burners on the floor a lone peanut was found. The questioning of the prep cooks revealed that a few of the kitchen staff were engaged in tossing peanuts up in the air and catching them in their mouths. They were sure they had accounted for every peanut that had missed. Obviously, with the peanut found by the stock burners and David's fatal reaction, they were wrong. One or more of the missed peanuts ended up in the soup and was pureed. David's autopsy showed no underlying physical infirmities that could have caused his death. The cause of death was determined to be complications from anaphylactic shock.

The Consequence:

David lost his life due to the senseless lapse of judgment and protocol by kitchen staff. While no one in the kitchen meant to hurt anyone, their game was deadly. The family, outraged by such activity, sought legal action against the restaurant and the facility. The family agreed to an out of court settlement with both the facility and the restaurant when they realized the suit would bankrupt both businesses. The family did not feel that David would want his death to put hundreds of families out of work. They knew this would not be a fitting tribute to their son's memory. Both businesses' insurance companies paid substantial settlements in addition to monies paid directly by the restaurant and the facility. The settlement will cost the restaurant and facility owners for many years. The kitchen staff involved in the incident lost their jobs and have to live with the senseless taking of David's life. Worst of all, David's family lost a much-loved son.

Big 8 Allergen

Tree Nuts

Food Allergy Safe
CASE STUDY: JOANNE

Background

Joanne was first diagnosed with tree nut allergies when she was about twelve years old. Her physician warned her that as an asthma sufferer, her reactions can be much more severe and dangerous. The physician prescribed a dual-dose EpiPen and stressed her need for no contact with the allergen. Joanne and her family learned the common names of tree nuts and diligently studied labels. They informed everyone connected with her food preparation of her tree nut allergy. All of their hard work paid off. Joanne went many years with not so much as a symptom of food allergy.

Now in her thirties, Joanne had a family of her own. Her asthma, once a regular attacker, had become only an occasional bother. Best of all Joanne hadn't had a tree nut allergic reaction since her first.

Event

One Sunday morning Joanne and her family attended a brunch at a restaurant she frequented for years. Much to her surprise, after about 30 minutes she started to demonstrate food reaction symptoms. Ever mindful of her physician's warning years ago Joanne immediately injected herself with her EpiPen. Her family transported her to the local emergency room where she was kept twelve hours for observation.

On Monday, Joanne returned to the restaurant and spoke to the manager. Despite everyone's best efforts, no source of the contaminate could be located. They ultimately chalked it up to some sort of inadvertent cross contamination.

Some weeks later Joanne ate at the restaurant again with a group of friends. Again she reacted and again she had to inject herself and go to the hospital. This time the restaurant manager went on a full-scale search for answers. Still, no one could find the source. Perplexed, the manager was chatting with their primary food purveyor representative and happened to mention the situation. The representative asked when the last time Joanne ate there without reaction and when her first reaction occurred. The manager obtained the information from Joanne and passed it on to his representative.

The next week when the food purveyor representative came in he had a list of all new or different items purchased by the restaurant since the last time Joanne ate without a reaction. One of the changes on the list corresponded with something Joanne ate both times she reacted. It seemed they had a new muffin supplier. Upon further investigation it was discovered that his muffins once packaged individually by type were now packaged in a variety pack. One of the muffins in the variety pack had almonds on top and was cross contaminating the other muffins in the pack.

The manager contacted Joanne and confirmed that almonds were the contaminate. Joanne was always careful to have her server bring muffins separate from the communal muffin basket. Though no one realized, with the change in supplier the muffins were coming in the door contaminated.

The Consequences:

Even though Joanne and the restaurant with her favorite brunch were very careful and each thought they were taking all necessary precautions to protect her, suppliers were not. The restaurant immediately discontinued purchasing those muffins despite their lower cost.
The muffin bakery was contacted by the purveyor and was unable to guarantee no cross contamination by tree nuts or peanuts. The purveyor dropped the bakery's product line from their offerings. The bakery was significantly impacted by this loss of a major portion of their business. They were so crippled by the loss that they had to substantially scale back their operation, and even with these moves nearly did not make it. Joanne had two brunches with two very expensive hospital trips and two costly uses of her EpiPens and two very miserable Sundays. With Joanne's other medical issues she was very lucky her reactions were not more severe. Both she and the restaurant know that the next time she might be less fortunate.

Big 8 Allergen

Fin Fish

Food Allergy Safe
CASE STUDY: HEATHER

Background

Heather is a forty-plus-year-old woman with a food allergy to fin fish. Heather is an informed diner and is careful to fully inform restaurant staff of her condition. Heather goes so far as to let them know to watch cooking surfaces and deep fryers and any other surface where fish may have come in contact. She further reminds servers about Caesar salad dressings with anchovies and to keep her salad well away.

Heather insists that all salad dressings be served on the side and that the dressing is pulled out of back stock using clean utensils. She further reminds them to use a fresh clean salad bowl if they toss the salad. She never orders soup with any seafood in it just in case fish stock may have been used.

Event

Heather attended an office luncheon at an upscale, well-known restaurant close to her work place. To ensure she got back within her lunch hour she asked about the soup and salad offering. Learning that the soup was cream of mushroom and the salad was a choice of tossed spring greens, Caesar or pasta salad, she placed an order for the soup and pasta salad. The wait person assured her the pasta salad was already tossed and did not contain any fish.

When the order arrived she began to enjoy her meal. Within minutes Heather began experiencing chest pains and shortness of breath. Before she could react she was unconscious. Her supervisor, aware of her allergy, dug in her purse and found her EpiPen and injected her. Paramedics were summoned and Heather was transported to the hospital. On the way Heather vomited in her oxygen mask and choked. The paramedics cleared her airway and restored her breathing. By the time they reached the emergency room Heather's blood pressure had dropped to dangerously low levels. Shortly after reaching the exam room Heather's heart stopped, with electric shock to her heart and drug injections she soon regained a heartbeat.

Days later Heather was discharged, sore from electric shocks and upset about the experience, she contacted the restaurant. They assured her no fish was in anything she ate. Since there was no doubt the reaction came from something in the restaurant she went in person to speak with management. They were not very helpful, even suggesting she encountered the allergen in something she had for breakfast. Discouraged, she contacted the corporate offices of the restaurant and spoke to management there. Again they were not helpful. They stuck to their story, telling her something else outside the restaurant must have made her sick. Heather was dumbfounded that neither manager had made any offer to attempt to investigate the incident that nearly took her life. Worse yet they were totally unconcerned. She knew it was just a matter of time before they killed someone.

CASE STUDY: HEATHER

Heather was not about to let it rest. She was determined to get answers. Heather engaged an attorney. Through the attorney's review of the restaurant records, which included all sales receipts for the day Heather had lunch, it was discovered that seafood chowder was also served that day. Through depositions from the employees, the legal team found out that seafood chowder left over from the day before was served to the early lunch crowd. However, by the time Heather got there the chowder had run out and cream of mushroom was served instead. Further testimony revealed that when the kitchen staff is busy, if the replacement soup is a cream-based soup and the previous soup is cream based they end up being mixed as the new soup is dumped in the same soup tureen for serving. This is exactly what happened the day Heather attended the luncheon there.

The Consequence:

Heather maintains that had management in either attempt made by her taken her issue seriously, she would not have retained an attorney. As it was, their behavior nearly cost Heather's life, and their callous lack of response and concern puts countless other people at risk. It is not known how many others were affected by this restaurant's practice nor is it known how many people made management aware of issues and were summarily dismissed and the issue ignored. It is known however that corporate had to pay expensive legal costs for Heather. They further paid for her medical bills, lost wages and pain and suffering. Most of these costs could have been avoided if someone had made an attempt to get to the bottom of Heather's incident. The managers involved placed the whole corporation at risk and as a result lost their jobs. Worst of all, Heather went through an unnecessary traumatic experience that could have taken her life and then was just brushed aside. The legal action was stressful and certainly not where Heather wanted to devote her time and money. Heather still asserts that despite her compensation she would not wish this experience on anyone.

Big 8 Allergen

Shell Fish

Food Allergy Safe
CASE STUDY: LESLIE

Background

Leslie was exposed to small amounts of shellfish as a child with never so much as a hint of a reaction. Later on in life as an adult Leslie noticed that sometimes when she consumed large amounts of shellfish she would become "flushed" on her neck and/or face. Leslie thought little of these occasional incidents until a trip to San Francisco where nearly every meal consumed over a week involved some sort of shellfish. After the sixth day her flush turned into a full-blown case of hives and she had to be treated with medication. Still Leslie just thought her issue was over consumption of a rich food.

Months later, when she consumed shellfish again, Leslie had a serious full anaphylactic reaction requiring a trip to the emergency room via ambulance. Frightened by the experience, Leslie visited her physician explaining all of the encounters she had with shellfish over the years. Her physician told Leslie how lucky she was that she had not experienced a severe reaction prior to this. All of her previous symptoms were precursors to a full anaphylactic reaction. Leslie left her physician's office with a prescription for an EpiPen and a strict set of orders not to have any contact with shellfish. Since then Leslie has been very careful to let servers know she cannot tolerate exposure to shellfish of any kind.

Event

Leslie has had considerable success in dining out until an outing where for no apparent reason she reacted. The restaurant immediately did the right thing and called for an aid car. Leslie spent the night and part of the next day in the hospital. Upon her release she phoned the restaurant to thank them for their quick response to her situation. In speaking to the general manager she was asked about her food order and the orders of the rest of the table in hopes the manager could determine the source of the shellfish.

Some days later a curious Leslie phoned the restaurant to inquire about the investigation. Much to her surprise the manager had indeed discovered the source of her reaction. It seems that the restaurant was serving shrimp bisque as their soup that day and that due to a nonfunctioning soup tureen the soup was transferred to the steam table. The condensate from the soup cross contaminated everything on the steam table including the potatoes she ate.

The Consequence:

Leslie experienced a frightening anaphylactic reaction along with another stay at a hospital. Leslie realizes that these reactions are life threatening and that the next one may be her last. She is painfully aware how exposed she is to the knowledge and understanding of food service personnel in the proper handling of food allergens. As always, along with the physical and mental toll these experiences have on her, there is also a substantial financial impact every time she is exposed.

Big 8 Allergen

Wheat

Food Allergy Safe
CASE STUDY: TAMMY

Background

Tammy and her husband had been saving for two years for a two-week dream winter vacation. Both she and her husband had not taken any time off for three years and with two young children the family was ready for some extended time away. Before they knew it plane tickets were purchased, ski resort rooms paid, rental car reserved and ski packages prepaid, and they were finally on their way.

Upon arrival at their well-known popular ski resort the family checked in, put their luggage away and headed downstairs to enjoy their first meal. Deciding to splurge the family bypassed the café and headed straight for fine dining.

Tammy, who is a food service professional employed as a waitperson in an upscale restaurant, suffers from celiac disease. Celiac disease is a degenerative condition which is triggered by the ingestion of gluten. Gluten is found among other sources in products with flour, barley or rye and their byproducts. The disease is eventually fatal if exposure to gluten is not completely eliminated. Exposure to gluten causes intense abdominal pain and extreme diarrhea. Symptoms can last from several days to a couple of weeks. Tammy, needless to say, is very careful about what she eats and never hesitates to inform restaurant staff of her issues. She even researches on-line for facilities that are food allergy friendly. Unfortunately these facilities are far and few between. As a food service professional, Tammy is well versed in kitchen operations and knows precisely what foods are "safe" for her to order.

Event

Before ordering Tammy asked for and spoke to the fine dining manager informing both him and the server of her condition. They both assured her that she was in fine dining and they were renowned for their attention to detail. Tammy ordered a salad and, renowned or not, she reminded them that the salad could not come in contact with any flour products so they must toss it in a washed, clean bowl and no croutons. The manager again assured her there would be no problem since the only salad they served with croutons was Caesar and she was not ordering one.

A few minutes later the family's food arrived and they began to enjoy their first meal on this wonderful, hard-earned vacation. Well over half way through her salad at the bottom of bowl Tammy came across a very large crouton. Horrified, Tammy immediately called over the manager who just minutes before assured her there would be no issue. Showing him the crouton Tammy asked if he had supervised the making of her salad as promised. He had to admit that he had not. The manager apologized profusely and said he would take the salad back and prepare it himself. Unfortunately it was too late. Through the tossing of the salad the crumbs off of the crouton were all through the salad and she had ingested them.

Worse yet, Tammy knew that as soon as the gluten entered her intestine she would be in great pain and be very ill for many days. In short, her vacation was over before it ever started.

The Consequence:

Tammy became acutely ill and required medical support along with IVs around the clock for several days. She was unable to function for over ten days, leaving her husband and children to fend for themselves. Everyone did all they could to make the best of the situation but between the pain and diarrhea it was miserable; made more so by the fact she was at a resort with none of the comforts of home, and it could have easily been prevented. Tammy sustained further damage to her intestine from the episode which she knows will cause her health to deteriorate. The resort felt terrible about her situation but only offered to pay for the family's accommodations. They did nothing to compensate her for medical bills or her loss of the vacation.

When it came time for the family to go home Tammy was unable to leave. Even with the medicine prescribed she could not sit on an airplane for an extended length of time, making travel impossible. Weakened and washed out several days later and alone, Tammy finally was well enough to go home. Their dream trip that took two years to save for became a two-week bad dream. Their financial loss was in the thousands. The extent of the physical damage she suffered and its impact on her health is unknown.

Big 8 Allergen

Soy

CASE STUDY: JIM

Background

Jim lives a very active life, with sports and all manner of outdoor activities a central part of his daily routine. Other than a few annual bouts of hay fever each year, Jim is an extremely healthy person. Jim could not have been happier when the "health food craze" started; he saw these foods as an enhancement to his already healthy lifestyle.

Jim immediately began making meatless and meat alternative choices in his diet. When enjoying meatless hot dogs and some meatless burgers, Jim began to notice a slight tingling sensation on his tongue. Gradually, additional mild physical responses began to appear. His fingers would tingle and he would notice some red blotchiness to his skin. None of these caused him much concern since he mainly noticed them while eating after somewhat strenuous activity.

Then on a group camping trip Jim's problems became much more pronounced with his tongue actually swelling. Jim had been fighting one of his annual hay fever attacks and was taking an antihistamine. Much to his surprise the drug seemed to ease this new symptom.

Upon his return home Jim went to his allergist and mentioned these strange and new symptoms he was experiencing. After some investigation it was discovered that Jim had an allergy to soy products. Jim was warned that the reactions were likely to increase in severity with each exposure. It was further explained that these reactions could be life threatening and that soy products were now strictly off limits.

Jim concerned as usual for his health, researched soy and familiarized himself with products that contained them. He learned to inform friends, family, delis, transportation companies, hotels and restaurants of his allergy. For the most part, other than a couple of cross contamination reactions traced backed to cooking surfaces, Jim pretty well managed his food allergy.

Event

With the onset of winter Jim and a group of his friends embarked on their big annual ski trip. Jim loved winter because hay fever was never a problem at this time of year. On the trip the group decided to eat at a much-loved restaurant. All ski trip participants had enjoyed this facility for many years and were extremely familiar with their menu. Despite this intimate knowledge they decided to be safe to let the manager and server know about Jim's allergy. They were assured that nothing on the menu contained soy or soy products.

Food Allergy Safe
CASE STUDY: JIM

The group ordered their dinners which came with a salad sprinkled with pine nuts. The salads arrived and the hungry diners cleaned their plates. Shortly thereafter the main course was delivered. As he began to eat Jim noticed the familiar tingling and began to feel flushed. He didn't feel this could be a reaction since really the only thing he had eaten was salad. Nonetheless Jim had some of his antihistamine with him and popped a couple. To Jim's surprise the drugs were not working as well as usual and as dinner progressed, Jim began to feel worse and worse. His friends, just to be on the safe side, talked him into a trip to the local emergency clinic.

Sure enough Jim's symptoms progressed and soon he was having a full-blown anaphylactic reaction. After a couple of epinephrine shots and IVs Jim was released 12 hours later. Returning to the lodge Jim did not feel well enough to ski and decided instead to rest. A few hours later Jim decided to head over to the restaurant and see if he could discover what in his food could have triggered his reaction.

The restaurant manager was helpful but could not fathom where the exposure could have come from. He happily called out the new kitchen manager to help in the inquiry. Much too everyone's surprise there was soy in Jim's food, but not in the main course which was pasta but on the salad. The kitchen manager explained that the increase in the cost of pine nuts prompted him to use toasted soy nuts instead. Unfortunately, he failed to inform anyone of the change and since Jim had never eaten toasted soy nuts he didn't recognize them.

The Consequence:

Jim felt under the weather for several days after his reaction. He did not feel well enough to ski until his last day of the trip. In addition to the $1,800.00 for his trip he had over $2,000.00 in emergency room expenses. Jim was kind enough not to ask the restaurant to cover any of these expenses but was quick to let them know if anything like this happened to him again because of their actions he would not be so nice. Upon Jim's return home his physician prescribed an EpiPen for Jim to carry on him at all times. Jim said this experience made him feel extremely vulnerable and literally at the mercy of the training of food service workers.

Big 9 Allergen

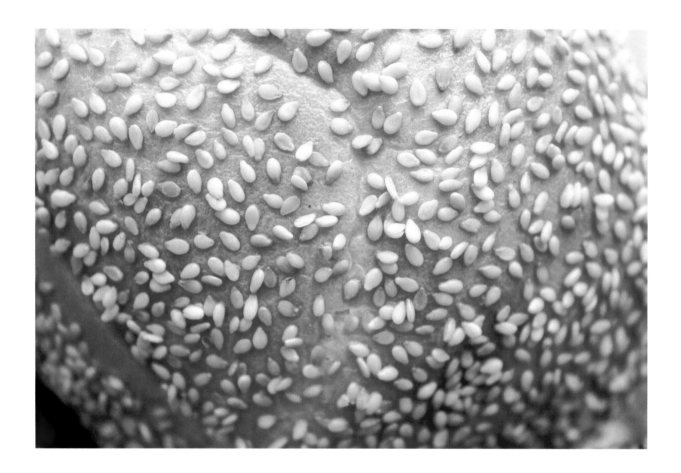

Sesame

Food Allergy Safe
CASE STUDY: ALLAN

Background

Allan found out early in life that he was allergic to sesame when as a toddler Allan got hold of a sesame breadstick. Growing up, Allan and his parents spent numerous hours in emergency rooms until they finally realized that hamburger restaurants, delis and bakeries were very dangerous places for Allan. Even his school cafeteria presented issues with sesame seed buns frequently used for their sandwich items.

As Allan matured, with the help of his physician, he and his parents were able to determine what foods and which restaurants he needed to avoid. His parents were diligent in their label reading and careful to inform friends, family, schools and eating establishments of his issues. For the most part, Allan's exposures to sesame came from cross contamination.

Fortunately, in all cases Allan had his EpiPen and other than the frightening experiences that anaphylactic reactions create, Allan led a fairly normal life.

Event

In his early thirties Allan's life could not have been going better. He had a wife, young children and a career he loved. When his company asked him and a number of his coworkers to attend a training program in another city he was thrilled. The majority of the group sent to the training program played on the company soft ball team which made the trip even more attractive. Allan's friends and his company were aware of his allergy and careful arrangements were made to ensure that Allan was safe in his food selections for the box lunches and the banquet on the last night.

The week went great, Allan and his friends/co-workers studied hard, passed the class and even managed to have some fun in the evenings. The night of the banquet all were enjoying themselves and when the dessert was served, a lovely gelato with an almond wafer, everybody was in high spirits, ready to go home the next morning. Allan, not wanting his wafer gave it to his friend and finished his gelato. Within a very few minutes Allan began to feel funny and turned to tell his friend, but before he could say anything he passed out on the floor. His friends, knowing about his allergy, felt around for his EpiPen and quickly found it in his jacket pocket on the back of his chair. Unfortunately, in the excitement his friend accidentally jabbed himself with the pen instead of Allan. Nothing was left to do but perform CPR and attempt to keep Allan alive until emergency services could arrive. Once paramedics were on the scene they took over CPR and transported Allan to the hospital. Unfortunately, the emergency personnel knew by Allan's condition that things did not look good and indeed they were not. It seems Allan's throat was swollen shut so the CPR that was administered did not provide enough oxygen to Allan's brain. Allan was profoundly brain damaged. Physicians kept him alive long enough for his wife and parents to arrive to say good-bye and he was removed from life support.

CASE STUDY: ALLAN

The Coroner's Office conducted an investigation into the incident with the assistance of the local health department. During their investigation all food handling personnel were questioned as well as attendees. No one could account for the sesame cross contamination.

Baffled, the investigators inspected the kitchen, prep areas and storage areas. During the inspection not one product with sesame in the ingredients could be located. Then in the pastry prep station a container of tahini (sesame paste) was discovered. The pastry chef was questioned and was adamant that he did not use the paste in his desserts and that the sesame paste was delivered by mistake. Investigators asked to see his staff schedule for the day the banquet food was prepared. On that day, due to high volume the pastry chef had assistance from staff outside of his department. When these people were interviewed it was discovered that when preparing the almond wafers, there was not enough almond paste and the prep-cook used "just a touch" of the sesame paste, "not enough that anyone would notice." The prep-cook was certain no one would be able to tell.

He was right no one could, except someone like Allan. What's more, how could it be an issue when everyone agreed that Allan didn't even eat his wafer!

The Consequences:

Allan lost his life when a prep-cook substituted what he considered an insignificant amount of an uncalled for ingredient. Because the amount was so small the taste could not be detected and without the prep-cook's disclosure of the substitution there was never a chance anyone would catch the error. Further the prep-cook was not trained to never deviate from recipe ingredients or to inform the chef if he did. Clearly from his response, he did not know that just a crumb from the wafer was enough to cause an allergic reaction and in this case the loss of Allan's life. Allan's company helped his family secure a substantial settlement from the restaurant/hotel even though their legal counsel attempted to mitigate their role by saying the friend actually caused his death by accidentally jabbing himself with Allan's EpiPen. Allan's employer did everything they could to inform the hotel of Allan's allergy; even Allan informed the hotel upon his arrival, but to no avail. Not only did the hotel suffer a monetary loss but they lost reputation and business as a result. They further lost when they dismissed the offending prep-cook and were required to pay for unlawful dismissal since the prep-cook was never trained in allergy safe food handling and had no idea of the consequences of his actions. Allan's company and co-workers lost a much appreciated employee and friend. Allan's wife and small children will live their lives without the support and love of a husband and father, something no amount of money can replace.

Food Allergy Safe
CASE STUDY: BRENDA

Background

Brenda was happy to accept a nice long weekend with friends at a lovely resort in the woods. The resort is a little over 48 miles from the nearest metropolitan area. On the way to the resort the group decided to stop and have dinner at a well-known upscale restaurant. The restaurant is part of a large chain and the group was familiar with both the menu and the location.

Brenda, who suffers from food allergies, intolerances and/or sensitivities, is quite accustomed to informing her server of her dietary restrictions. This visit was no different. The menu featured a pasta dish described as topped with red peppers. Brenda inquired whether the peppers were actually cooked in the sauce or were they simply a topping as described. The wait person confirmed the peppers were just a topping and they could be "easily left off." Brenda went ahead and ordered the dish emphasizing her allergy to peppers to which the wait person replied "no problem."

Event

After a few minutes the food order for the table arrived and much to everyone's shock Brenda's dish was covered in red peppers. Brenda patiently explained to the server again that she was allergic to red peppers. The wait person apologized explaining she "asked" the kitchen to hold the peppers and immediately removed the plate taking it back to the kitchen. Minutes later the order reappeared and was placed in front of Brenda. One look at the plate and it was apparent that despite efforts to disguise the fact, this was the same plate with the offending allergen picked off.

Frustrated, Brenda again summoned the wait person, and Brenda again explained that she had a food allergy and merely removing the allergen is not sufficient. The whole plate was contaminated by the original peppers and that if she consumed the pasta she would become very ill. The wait person again apologized explaining she thought that the removal of the peppers would suffice. It was explained to the server that the order would have to be remade and a fresh plate prepared. Meanwhile Brenda sat and watched everyone else dine on food that had become cold while waiting for her meal to be re-presented the first time. Finally, her dinner arrived and she consumed it while the others at the table, who had already finished with their own food, waited.

The Consequence:

Brenda and the restaurant were very lucky that the kitchen had not done a better job of disguising the fact that the original order was not remade. The pasta when re-presented had been re-tossed and either when they were dumping it back in the pan or back in the bowl the sauce splattered off of the noodles under the edge of the bowl. If this had gone unnoticed by Brenda or if it had been wiped off by kitchen or wait staff she would have consumed the allergen. Brenda would have first developed an itchy rash and indigestion; sometime later nausea would set in. Still later she would experience vomiting and diarrhea all lasting from hours to days. All of this leaving her extremely dehydrated and in need of medical support which at her remote resort location was unavailable. Not only would she experience medical expenses but she and the group would lose the monies paid for the extended weekend. Had her reaction gone even further, Brenda was over 48 miles from the nearest medical help, leaving her extremely vulnerable. As anyone with food allergy issues knows, reactions can turn dangerous and even deadly very quickly. Needless to say the ruined weekend for the party pales in comparison to physical, mental and financial impact a reaction would have had on Brenda. As for the restaurant, with the lack of knowledge demonstrated by the server it is only a matter of time before someone is not as lucky as Brenda. There is of course no predicting the impact to the guest and to the establishment when this happens.

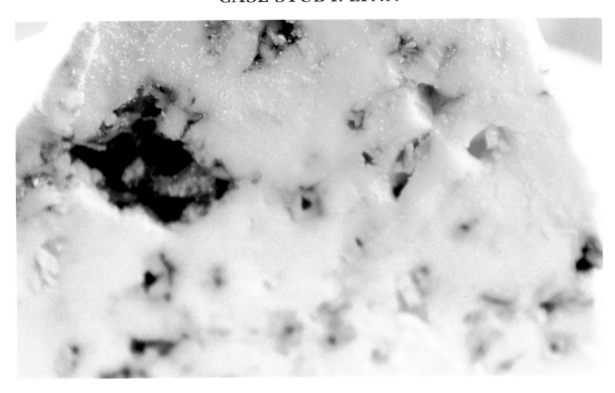

Background

Lynn grew up eating pretty much anything put in front of her. From a very young age she enjoyed a wide variety of foods. Living in very large cosmopolitan areas all over the nation she experienced food fare from a number of countries and ethnic backgrounds. She had no known allergies of any type.

In her early twenties she had a severe reaction to penicillin, a drug she had successfully taken for many years. The reaction was a full-blown anaphylactic reaction and required hospitalization. After she recovered she was instructed by her physician never to take the drug in any form again.

Event

Months later Lynn went to her favorite steak house for her birthday dinner. With her selection Lynn ordered a salad with her salad dressing of choice for many years, blue cheese. Lynn consumed blue cheese dressing on a fairly regular basis without incident. This occasion however was different; within minutes of consuming her salad she began to develop severe hives, nausea and swelling of the face tongue and throat.

CASE STUDY: LYNN

Fortunately, one of the members of her birthday party was a physician and recognized this as an anaphylactic reaction. His quick reaction was all that saved her life. After another stay in the hospital she was told to stay away from any cheese with a blue line in it.

The Consequence:

Years later and after several more reactions she discovered that not only was she allergic to blue-lined cheese and penicillin but any mold on foods. She further discovered that a very tiny amount of the allergen or something as insignificant as a smear off of a utensil or hand is enough to cause a reaction and that cooking does not prevent a reaction.

Since then she has been poisoned through direct and cross contamination by restaurants, delis, buffets, parties and picnics. When informing wait staff or other food service workers of her allergy she has listened to them say things like "oh boy we've got a picky one on table such and such." These comments came in spite of her explanation that exposure to the allergen can cause her death. Carelessness and blatant disregard has hospitalized her many times.

Lynn's exposure to her allergen by food-service workers has cost her tens of thousands of dollars in medical bills over the years. She has missed many days of work and had more ruined special events than she cares to recall. Many times it has just been luck that she did not suffer severe permanent damage or lose her life. Lynn has a great respect and eye for the important and critical role food-service individuals can and do play in the health of the general public. Near-death experiences are devastating and are the primary reason she wrote this training program.

CASE STUDY: THE RESTAURANT

CASE STUDY: THE RESTAURANT

Background

A well run and respected restaurant located in a lovely facility and beautiful setting booked a holiday party for 80 plus people. The company booking the party is a large sales firm very active in the greater community. The management and owners of the sales firm are very familiar with the high quality and excellent reputation of this long-established restaurant. For their holiday party the firm requested a choice of prime rib and salmon. Approximately 35 of the attendees chose the salmon with the rest selecting the prime rib.

The eating establishment ordered everything for the party from their primary purveyor, a company they have conducted business with and enjoyed an excellent relationship with for many years. The food was delivered the day of the event with the salmon in two large filets able to serve all 35 people. Preparation of the meal was handled by their long-time kitchen manager and head chef.

Event

The event went on as scheduled with all participants pleased with the presentation, quality, taste and portion of the dinner. The excellent service, beautiful setting and warm surroundings capped off the affair, causing the sales firm to declare the evening a complete success. That was until the next day when some of the firm's employees contacted the owners complaining they became ill, a couple of whom ended up in the emergency room. It was discovered all of the individuals who were ill ate the salmon.

The sales firm owners contacted the restaurant owner to inform him of the issue. The restaurant owner contacted everyone who ate the salmon only to discover that the only people who became ill were the few already reported. This made no sense since all of the individuals who ate salmon ate off the same filets. It stood to reason that if a few were sick all should be ill but that was not the case. Since the fish was fresh, and was handled and prepared by an expert, the whole incident made no sense.

The restaurant owner, baffled and unable to come up with any answers, contacted his purveyor to see if it could shed any light on the situation. As it turned out the purveyor was able to research the incident and came up with an explanation. In an effort to keep the pricing and portion size where the sales organization requested, ranch-raised salmon instead of fresh wild salmon was ordered. Unfortunately, unknown to the restaurant owner, ranch salmon are fed a pellet that contains a dye to turn the flesh pink and approximately 1 to 3% of the population reacts negatively to this dye. Oddly enough, the number of participants made ill reflected this statistic exactly.

Food Allergy Safe
CASE STUDY: THE RESTAURANT

The Consequence:

The restaurant owner shared his findings with the sales organization owner explaining he was completely unaware of the dye issue and in fact he had never heard of it. The restaurant refunded all monies spent on the event and apologized. Everyone seemed to understand and was satisfied with the explanation and the refund. Reality, however, proved to be much different. The restaurant owner once enjoyed frequent business from the company's owners and employees. Since the incident he has not seen a single person from their organization. Even individuals who had been long-time guests have not returned. Not only did the restaurant lose all of the revenue from the party and have to come out-of-pocket for the food, labor and supplies, they lost all future business from the 80 plus participants. Additionally, their reputation with these 80 plus people is ruined as well as with the people they tell. The restaurant suffered a tarnished reputation through no fault of their own, other than ignorance of a feed additive that can effect humans. The major positive to the situation was that although people became ill, no one lost their life. This would have been entirely possible if an individual with a compromised physical constitution had gotten ill.

RESPONSIBILITIES OF THE INDIVIDUAL

No matter what duties a person performs in an establishment that handles food for public consumption, the need to understand food allergy, food intolerance and food sensitivity issues is primary. Even if the person does not directly handle food, they likely are involved in cleaning the surfaces and implements which the food or food-sensitive people will come in contact with. They may take to-go orders or solely prepare drinks or seat people. Regardless of position, all must know what to do and how their individual actions may affect the public.

Your food allergy reaction avoidance responsibilities as a food service worker are:

1. Know your company's food allergy handling, protocols, policies and procedures regardless of whether you handle food directly or not.

2. Never tell a guest if something does or does not contain a specific ingredient unless you KNOW FOR SURE. Remember recipes change and you may not be aware of the change.

3. If you don't know say so!

4. Always refer a food allergy question to the manager or supervisor on duty.

5. Know who to ask if your manager or supervisor is unavailable.

RESPONSIBILITIES OF THE INDIVIDUAL

Cleaning

1. Clean all surfaces thoroughly with appropriate sanitizers and rinse the cleaning cloth in the sanitizer bucket between each table or area.

2. Wash all implements in the dishwasher, wiping out or rinsing off is not enough to eliminate allergens.

3. Clean menus and menu covers frequently with sanitizer. This will prevent food residue from previous diners from affecting food sensitive individuals.

IF...

- If you are not food allergy safe certified, always refer a takeout order to the manager or supervisor once you are informed the guest has a special food handling need.

- If you are packing a takeout order make sure you check to see if there are any special handling instructions.

- If you see or are accidentally involved in a food allergy contamination or cross-contamination incident, pull the contaminated food or implements immediately, then report it to your management. It is not worth destroying your business or harming your guests.

- If a guest tells you they have a food handling issue make sure their server and the supervisor or manager on duty know.

- If you see objects on the floor or under a table that don't belong there – pick them up. Remember children will often crawl under tables or pick things up off the floor. Again, food residue can be a real danger for a food sensitive child.

- If you see anything mishandled with regard to food allergy safe handling report it immediately.

- If a guest tells you they have a food issue, believe them!

General Information

Never view guests with special food handling needs as picky or overly demanding. Remember, a mistake by you or your co-workers could cost them their life.

Be mindful of where your hands have been, you touch many of the same surfaces your food sensitive guests do and for some food residue is a very real issue.

RESPONSIBILITIES OF THE INDIVIDUAL

Familiarize yourself with what questions to ask if a guest informs you of a food issue while making reservations or a to-go order.

Always treat special food handling requests as if they are allergies. Sometimes individuals with food allergies do not understand that just asking for something to be held or left off will not protect them.

- Know and understand your organization's food allergy handling protocols, procedures and processes. If in doubt ask your manager before you act.

- Be aware of what is in your area and how it is handled. If you see something directly or cross contaminated remove it immediately and inform your manager.

As a valuable member of staff, your compliance to allergy safe food handling protocols, policies and procedures is critical.

Allergy Reactions

- In case of a food allergy reaction, **always call** 911 or your emergency services.

- Know the address and phone number of the restaurant and be sure to tell them it is a suspected food allergy reaction.

- Remember in a crisis we tend to become flustered and may forget simple things like the address and phone number, so have a cheat sheet posted or clearly visible near the phone.

- Letting the emergency services know that it is a suspected food allergy reaction will allow them to dispatch the appropriate personnel. Not all emergency personnel carry or are authorized to administer the drugs necessary to combat the reaction.

AND NEVER HESITATE to call emergency services, MINUTES COUNT!

Lastly, be mindful of your personal conduct, even the smallest prank or lapse in judgment may prove very harmful to one of your guests.

FOOD ALLERGY SAFE HANDLING RESPONSIBILITIES OF A HOST OR HOSTESS

Reservations

When a host or a hostess is informed of a food allergy issue by a guest or office of a reservation book notation he or she should:

1. Table Assignment
Identify and reserve a table for the guest as far away from the kitchen as possible and let other servers know you have a guest with a food allergy issue at that table. This will prevent the guest from coming in contact with food vapors from the kitchen and let other servers know to steer a wide path when delivering steaming or sizzling plates.

2. Allergy Alert
When taking reservations, be sure to **clearly note and noticeably mark** the allergy alert. Guests may assume because they already told you while making the reservation that everyone will be aware of their needs and not reiterate the issue.

3. Large Party
When booking a large party be sure to ask if anyone has any food or special handling issues. The individual booking the party may not know, however your question may prompt them to ask and let you know.

FOOD ALLERGY SAFE HANDLING RESPONSIBILITIES OF A HOST OR HOSTESS

Seating

1. Before seating the guest, clean:

- The table (including the edges and underneath), be sure to check under the table, if there are any foreign objects remove them
- Chairs, booth seats & backs, benches
- Decorations, candle holders
- Condiment containers
- Menus
- Supply the table with new unused crayons if you offer them or have them on the table
- Inform the server, bus person and manager on duty. This will ensure no one will inadvertently contaminate anything brought to the table and give the manager an opportunity to visit with the guest and inform the kitchen of the impending special handling order.

Be sure to use a fresh cleaning cloth soaked in the sanitizer bucket. These actions will prevent allergen contact from food residue left by previous diners.

2. Menu Selections

Never make menu selection recommendations. Leave this to the manager, chef or server. This will prevent you from making the wrong recommendation. Remember recipes and ingredients change and you may not have been informed.

3. Check Presentation

- If you handle the check presentation or payment, clean the guest check folder or check tray before presentation. Be sure to use a cloth out of the sanitizer bucket, this will prevent food residue contact from the previous handlers.
- Be sure complimentary mints or after dinner sweets come out of a fresh non-public contact supply. This will prevent contamination from hands in the working supply.

FOOD ALLERGY SAFE HANDLING RESPONSIBILITIES OF A HOST OR HOSTESS

As a valuable member of staff, your compliance to allergy safe food handling protocols, policies and procedures is critical.

Allergy Reactions

- In case of a food allergy reaction, **always call** 911 or your emergency services.

- Know the address and phone number of the restaurant and be sure to tell them it is a suspected food allergy reaction.

- Remember in a crisis we tend to become flustered and may forget simple things like the address and phone number, so have a cheat sheet posted or clearly visible near the phone.

- Letting the emergency services know that it is a suspected food allergy reaction will allow them to dispatch the appropriate personnel. Not all emergency personnel carry or are authorized to administer the drugs necessary to combat the reaction.

AND NEVER HESITATE to call emergency services, MINUTES COUNT!

Lastly, be mindful of your personal conduct, even the smallest prank or lapse in judgment may prove very harmful to one of your guests.

FOOD ALLERGY SAFE HANDLING RESPONSIBILITIES OF BUS PERSONNEL

When bus personnel are made aware of a guest with a food allergy issue he or she should:

1. Cleaning

- Before the guest is seated – with a fresh cloth from the sanitizer bucket thoroughly clean the table (including edges & underneath), chairs, booth seats & backs, benches, condiment containers, decorations, candles, the wall along the table, in short anything the guest might touch. Check under the table and remove any foreign materials. This will prevent food residue contact from previous diners.

- If there is a spill be sure to soak it up from the carpet and other soft surfaces. Be sure to wipe off around and underneath edges with a fresh cloth from the sanitizer bucket. This will prevent contact with food residue by children who go under tables and adults who put purses, bags and backpacks on the floor.

FOOD ALLERGY SAFE HANDLING RESPONSIBILITIES OF BUS PERSONNEL

Setting the Table

- When setting a table for a food allergy guest always take napkins, place mats, table cloths, utensils and bread plates from further down in the stack. This will prevent cross-contaminated items from making their way to the table.

- Wipe off with a fresh cloth from the sanitizer bucket common-use items you bring to the table such as ketchup, mustard, jelly jars, baskets, steak sauces, etc. Again, this prevents food residue from previous diners.

Serving the Guest

- Before bringing anything to the table wash your hands! Remember you handle a lot of dirty plates, cups, glasses, silverware, napkins, place mats, wrappers and more. If your hands are not washed you may be the source of food residue from previous diners.

- Never bring anything new to the table unless you check with server. The item requested by anyone other than the manager or server may contain an allergen you are unaware of.

- If you bring crayons to the table be sure they are new. Used crayons may contain food residue from previous guests.

- If you bring complimentary after-dinner mints or sweets be sure they are out of a fresh non-public-contact supply. This will prevent transference of food residue from outside sources.

Menu Selections

- Never make menu selection recommendations. Leave this to the manager, chef or server. This will prevent you from making the wrong recommendation. Remember recipes and ingredients change and you may not have been informed.

Accidents Happen

If you see or are accidentally involved in a food allergy contamination or cross contamination pull the contaminated food or implements immediately and report the incident to your manager. It is not worth destroying your business or harming your guests.

FOOD ALLERGY SAFE HANDLING RESPONSIBILITIES OF BUS PERSONNEL

As a valuable member of staff, your compliance to allergy safe food handling protocols, policies and procedures is critical.

Allergy Reactions

- In case of a food allergy reaction, **always call** 911 or your emergency services.

- Know the address and phone number of the restaurant and be sure to tell them it is a suspected food allergy reaction.

- Remember in a crisis we tend to become flustered and may forget simple things like the address and phone number, so have a cheat sheet posted or clearly visible near the phone.

- Letting emergency services know that it is a suspected food allergy reaction will allow them to dispatch the appropriate personnel. Not all emergency personnel carry or are authorized to administer the drugs necessary to combat the reaction.

AND NEVER HESITATE to call emergency services, MINUTES COUNT!

Lastly, be mindful of your personal conduct, even the smallest prank or lapse in judgment may prove very harmful to one of your guests.

FOOD ALLERGY SAFE HANDLING RESPONSIBILITIES OF SERVERS

FOOD ALLERGY SAFE HANDLING RESPONSIBILITIES OF SERVERS

When a server is made aware of a guest with a food allergy he or she should:

Table Assignment

Seat the guest as far away from the kitchen as possible and let other servers know you have a guest with a food allergy issue at that table. This will prevent the guest from coming in contact with food vapors from the kitchen and let other servers know to steer a wide path when delivering steaming or sizzling plates.

Setting/Serving the Table

a. Be sure the table (including edges & underneath), chairs, booth seats & backs, benches, condiment containers, wall next to the table, candles, decorations or anything a guest might come in contact with is thoroughly cleaned with a fresh cloth soaked in the sanitizer bucket. This will prevent contact with food residue from previous guests.

b. Wash your hands before bringing the table anything. Remember you handle a number of plates, cups, glasses, etc., all of which may contain your guest's food allergen residue.

c. Clean menus thoroughly with a fresh cloth out of the sanitizer bucket before handing them to the guest. This will prevent contamination from food residue left by previous guests and co-workers.

d. If you provide crayons for children or young-at-heart guests be sure they are new. This will prevent contamination from food residue left by previous guests.

e. Inform your team you have someone with a food allergy issue. This forewarns others of a special handling order and allows others to focus on your food allergy safe protocols, policies and procedures.

f. Never view guests with food allergies as picky or difficult. Remember, food allergy intolerances and sensitivities can be life threatening.

g. When speaking to guests about their food issues, listen carefully and take notes. Many times the guest will be very helpful in helping you and the chef determine easy food selection alternatives.

h. Be honest with your guests, if you DON'T KNOW something tell them. Do not guess, if you are wrong they are sick or dead.

i. Always believe the guest when they tell you they have a food issue. Think of other places where the allergen might hide. Watch out for beverages that may contain the allergen and be aware of items that might have come in contact with items you are serving.

FOOD ALLERGY SAFE HANDLING RESPONSIBILITIES OF SERVERS

Order Taking

a. Listen carefully to any guest who asks you to hold something on a dish. Be sure the hold is a preference not an allergy. Some guests will merely ask you to hold something rather than disclose the allergy.

b. Be sure to let your special handling guest know if the kitchen is overwhelmed and a particular dish is likely to be mishandled; steer them toward something safe. Most guests will thank you for it!

c. Once you are clear about the guest's food issue, speak to the chef and your manager before making menu recommendations. Remember recipes and ingredients change and you may not be aware of the change.

d. Always put the allergen on the kitchen order even if the guest is not ordering something with the allergen in it. This will prevent accidental contamination from something in the kitchen and it warns the kitchen in case there is a hidden allergen in something ordered.

e. Never just put "hold the _____" (allergen) on the order. The kitchen has no way of knowing if this guest has an allergy or simply doesn't care for the ingredient. This exposes the guest to direct and cross contamination.

f. Always noticeably mark or flag the order and the allergen. This will allow the special handling order to stick out from all of the other orders.

g. Let the kitchen know the special handling order is coming. If you have to, have the manager inform the kitchen. Some kitchens prohibit or limit call-in or verbal instructions from the floor staff. If this is the case in your operation, speak either to the kitchen manager or restaurant manager.

h. Be sure you work out with the management and the kitchen staff a segregated place to pick up the order and who will deliver it to the table. Be sure everyone knows not to touch or handle the order unless instructed to do so. This will prevent spills, splatters, steam, vapor, bumping and hand cross contamination.

i. Be sure to let your expeditor know you have a special handling order and who will be picking the order up.

j. If the special order contains the allergen or has become cross contaminated it MUST BE REFIRED. Under no circumstances pick out, scrape off, wipe off or remove the allergen. Do not allow anyone else to do so either. DO NOT SERVE THE DISH UNTIL IT IS REMADE. Remember even the tiniest amount of the allergen can trigger a life threatening reaction. If there is an issue with the remake, take the dish to your manager and let them handle it. The guest has placed their trust in you, you must protect them!

k. Always deliver the special order separately from all other plates, including the rest of the order on the table. Be sure if a tray is used the tray has been thoroughly cleaned with a fresh cloth from the sanitizer bucket and that there is nothing else on the tray other than the special handling plate. This will prevent cross contamination from other dishes that might splash, spill or touch the order.

l. After the table is served allow the guest to inspect and review the plate. Don't leave until they have approved the dish. If there is a problem you can respond immediately.

m. Ideally, any common-use condiments such as ketchup, mustard, steak sauces, jelly/jam jars, baskets, etc., are new when served to your special handling guest. If that is not possible, using a fresh cloth from the sanitizer bucket thoroughly clean the item before taking it to the table. This will prevent food residue contact left by previous guests.

n. Before presenting the guest check be sure to thoroughly clean the check folder or tray with a fresh cloth soaking in the sanitizer bucket. This prevents food residue contact from previous guests.

o. If you serve after-dinner mints or sweets be sure they are from a fresh supply that has not had previous public or co-worker contact. This prevents food residue contact from the hands of others.

General Information

a. Know and understand your organization's food allergy handling protocols, procedures and processes. If in doubt ask your manager before you act.

b. Be aware of what is in your area and how it is handled. If you see something directly or cross contaminated remove it immediately and inform your manager.

FOOD ALLERGY SAFE HANDLING RESPONSIBILITIES OF SERVERS

As a valuable member of staff, your compliance to allergy safe food handling protocols, policies and procedures is critical.

Allergy Reactions

- In case of a food allergy reaction, **always call** 911 or your emergency services.

- Know the address and phone number of the restaurant and be sure to tell them it is a suspected food allergy reaction.

- Remember in a crisis we tend to become flustered and may forget simple things like the address and phone number, so have a cheat sheet posted or clearly visible near the phone.

- Letting emergency services know that it is a suspected food allergy reaction will allow them to dispatch the appropriate personnel. Not all emergency personnel carry or are authorized to administer the drugs necessary to combat the reaction.

AND NEVER HESITATE to call emergency services, MINUTES COUNT!

Lastly, be mindful of your personal conduct, even the smallest prank or lapse in judgment may prove very harmful to one of your guests.

FOOD ALLERGY SAFE HANDLING RESPONSIBILITIES OF THE DISH WASHER

The dish washer is an important and integral component in the food allergy safe program. Since this position "touches" nearly everything that is used in the kitchen and most things used to serve in the front of the house, they must be especially diligent at all times. To prevent food allergy reactions the dish washer should:

1. Be mindful of what is on your hands and gloves when handling clean items. Casual food residue contact can easily be transferred to the outside, handles and edges of clean items.

2. If an item comes in contact through splashing, splattering, touching or setting down where food residue may reside, even if it is on the outside or bottom of the item, it must be REWASHED. Simply wiping off will not remove food residue, and restocking the item will further contaminate whatever it comes in contact with.

3. Never just "rinse off" a pan, bowl, cookie sheet, etc., because it will be heated. Heat does not kill the proteins responsible for allergic reactions.

4. Use fresh towels from the sanitizer bucket. Hanging a towel off of the waist and using it over and over to clean surfaces without soaking in the sanitizer bucket will do nothing but spread food residue, contaminates and germs all over these surfaces.

Stocking

a. When stocking clean items be careful where they are set when replenishing bins or racks, or when stacking takes place. For example: a counter with flour on it will contaminate the

FOOD ALLERGY SAFE HANDLING RESPONSIBILITIES
OF THE DISH WASHER

bottom of a plate thereby causing cross contamination of the eating surface of the plate on which it is stacked.

b. When removing items from a buffet or salad bar do not drip or splatter other items with what is being removed. This will cross contaminate the remaining items. If this should occur, remove the contaminated items and inform the manager. Remember scraping off, picking or spooning out does not eliminate contaminants.

c. When removing dirty items from any food line do not set utensils in other containers with food in them. This will prevent cross contamination.

d. Be careful when using tongs or other devices to remove pans or containers from buffets, salad bars and food lines. Be sure not to set them in anything that has food in it and do not set them on surfaces on which other foods, hands or clean items will come in contact. This will prevent cross contamination.

e. Never handle or carry clean items by the food or drink contact surfaces. Silverware, kitchen utensils and glasses are especially easy to grab by the business end and, while it is agreed this is a general health issue, to many food allergy sufferers it can be deadly.

f. Clean screens and filters on dishwasher frequently. This will prevent food residue from coming in contact with clean items. To prevent contamination check dishwasher solutions, indicator lights, and dishwasher basin for food chunks and pieces.

General Information

a. If you see or are accidentally involved in any incident that causes the contamination or cross contamination of anything the guest might come in contact with, remove the affected items and report it to your manager immediately.

b. Know and understand your organization's food allergy handling protocols, procedures, and processes. If in doubt ask your manager before you act.

c. Be aware of what is in your area and how it is handled. If you see something directly or cross contaminated remove it immediately and inform your manager.

FOOD ALLERGY SAFE HANDLING RESPONSIBILITIES
OF THE DISH WASHER

As a valuable member of staff, your compliance to allergy safe food handling protocols, policies and procedures is critical.

Allergy Reactions

- In case of a food allergy reaction, **always call** 911 or your emergency services.

- Know the address and phone number of the restaurant and be sure to tell them it is a suspected food allergy reaction.

- Remember in a crisis we tend to become flustered and may forget simple things like the address and phone number, so have a cheat sheet posted or clearly visible near the phone.

- Letting emergency services know that it is a suspected food allergy reaction will allow them to dispatch the appropriate personnel. Not all emergency personnel carry or are authorized to administer the drugs necessary to combat the reaction.

AND NEVER HESITATE to call emergency services, MINUTES COUNT!

Lastly, be mindful of your personal conduct, even the smallest prank or lapse in judgment may prove very harmful to one of your guests.

FOOD ALLERGY SAFE HANDLING RESPONSIBILITIES OF CHEFS AND COOKS

Preparing the Order

When the kitchen receives an order with a food allergy alert or flag it should:

1. Believe the guest when they say they have an allergy. Don't view them as just another picky customer. This assumption can and will eventually harm a guest.

2. Inform other kitchen staff that you have a special handling order. This will put them on alert and allow them to exercise special care.

3. Determine who will follow the dish through the entire preparation process. With one person in charge the chance of error is greatly reduced.

4. Review the order to be sure there are no hidden allergens in any part of the dish.

5. If the dish contains ingredient components that you do not know the contents of via conventional labeling standards, then ask the guest to select another dish.

FOOD ALLERGY SAFE HANDLING RESPONSIBILITIES OF CHEFS AND COOKS

Food Prep

- Once the final selection has been made review the order to determine if in the preparation process the food will come in contact with a known contaminate.
  - Will something on the plate be deep fried in oil where the offending allergen will have deposited proteins that are not destroyed, causing cross contamination? For example: will French fries be cooked in the same oil as shrimp?
  - Will something on their plate come off of a steam table where the offending allergen may be held, allowing vapor and condensate to cross contaminate the order?

- Review all labels for the ingredients of the dish from all suppliers.

- Remember suppliers change their recipes too.

- Review your own recipes, making sure your ingredients have not changed.

- If you are unsure of any ingredient let the server, manager and guest know the dish may not be safe. Help guide them to a safe dish.

Cooking/Cleaning

a. Before starting the dish be sure all surfaces, utensils, pots & pans, mixing bowls, staging surfaces, plates, and anything else their food will come in contact with are clean and free of the allergen. Never just rinse off, wipe off or scrape off surfaces, this will not rid the area of allergens. They must be washed with sanitizer.

b. During preparation be sure to segregate the order from allergens that can splash, splatter, drip or otherwise come in contact with the order.

c. Plate the food on a plate fresh out of the dishwasher. This will prevent use of a plate off the line which may have become cross contaminated.

d. Use utensils fresh from the dishwasher.

e. Your hands and gloves must be clean.

f. Do not let anyone else garnish the dish and be sure to use garnish from a fresh back-stock supply. This will ensure the garnish will not have been cross contaminated.

FOOD ALLERGY SAFE HANDLING RESPONSIBILITIES
OF CHEFS AND COOKS

g. Once completed immediately deliver the plate to the manager, server or the guest. If that is not possible segregate the plate well away from all other plates to ensure it cannot come in contact with the allergen.

h. If you remotely suspect contamination or if an error has been made do not pick out, peel off, scrape off, or wipe away the allergen. REMAKE THE DISH! Remember the slightest, tiniest speck of the allergen may be enough to trigger an allergic reaction or death.

i. If the server brings the dish back because of a mishap on their end you must REMAKE the dish – no exception! Failure to do so gambles with your guest's life.

j. Remember the only treatment for food allergies, intolerances and sensitivities is strict NO CONTACT with the offending food.

k. If you don't know or are unsure of anything that has to do with the safety of the guest, say so. They will thank you for it. Remember they have placed their trust in you, you must protect them.

l. When removing containers from the hot or cold line or from buffets and salad bars be sure that serving utensils are not placed in other containers with food in them elsewhere on the serving line which will contaminate a dish. Often contaminated in this manner are items we are accustomed to using multiple times without washing, such as spoons, ladles, tongs and thermometers.

m. The dredging bowl or pan if used for multiple foods becomes the source of contamination.

n. Never use cookie sheets, pots and pans, mixing bowls, rolling pins, etc., without washing them in between food changes; they must be washed with sanitizer.

o. When flouring items, be sure plates, surfaces and other foods will not be accidentally dusted. If dusted, they must be thoroughly washed, sanitized or remade.

p. If you see or are accidentally involved with contaminating anything, pull the item immediately. It is not worth destroying your business or harming your guests.

FOOD ALLERGY SAFE HANDLING RESPONSIBILITIES
OF CHEFS AND COOKS

q. Be mindful of your apron and the towel hanging from your waistband or lying on the counter; these are good sources of cross contamination.

r. When replenishing stock on the hot or cold line be careful not to spill or splash into other foods.

s. Never use the same utensil to transfer multiple foods without washing it in between foods.

t. Be aware heat does not kill the proteins that trigger allergic reactions, only washing and sanitizing will.

u. Be mindful of how ready-made foods are packaged and stored when they are delivered to your establishment. For example, if you purchase ready-made brownies, some with nuts and some without, be sure they are not in direct contact with each other.

Policy, Protocol & Procedures

1. When foods are repackaged at your facility, ensure they do not come in contact with other foods that contain known allergens.

2. Constantly review ingredient labels on items purchased from purveyors. They, like you, will change recipes.

3. Familiarize yourself with the numerous names for the same ingredient. If you encounter an ingredient you can't identify, contact your supplier, they will find out for you.

4. Know the "Big 8 Allergens & Sesame" and look for where they hide. Many will be in places you don't suspect. You are your establishment's food expert; if you don't know, no one else will.

5. There is no such thing as a secret recipe or ingredient when it comes to food allergies, intolerances and sensitivities. You must disclose if the offending allergen is in the food. You must also make your staff aware of the ingredients so they can safely serve guests.

6. When you change a recipe **EVERYONE** on staff must be alerted. Incorrect information endangers your guests and your establishment.

FOOD ALLERGY SAFE HANDLING RESPONSIBILITIES OF CHEFS AND COOKS

7. Alert **EVERYONE** when you have substituted ingredients, particularly if they are one of the "Big 8 Allergens or Sesame." Your regular guests with food issues are especially vulnerable when you substitute an ingredient, since they have enjoyed your dishes in the past without any problems and assume them to be safe.

8. Post a reference guide for your kitchen staff containing the ingredients in all of your dishes. Notate them when they contain one of the "Big 8 Allergens or Sesame." Don't forget your specials and daily soups.

9. Don't be fooled by the terms: non-dairy, egg substitute, imitation_____ , etc. Many of these contain some form of the ingredient they claim not to. If you are not sure about a product, find out from your supplier or the manufacturer. **Educate all staff.**

10. Know and understand your organization's food allergy safe handling protocols, policies and procedures. If you have input to improve or streamline the food allergy safe handling protocols, policies and procedures, share it with staff and management.

As a valuable member of staff, your compliance to allergy safe food handling protocols, policies and procedures is critical.

Allergy Reactions

- In case of a food allergy reaction, **always call** 911 or your emergency services.

- Know the address and phone number of the restaurant and be sure to tell them it is a suspected food allergy reaction.

- Remember in a crisis we tend to become flustered and may forget simple things like the address and phone number, so have a cheat sheet posted or clearly visible near the phone.

- Letting emergency services know that it is a suspected food allergy reaction will allow them to dispatch the appropriate personnel. Not all emergency personnel carry or are authorized to administer the drugs necessary to combat the reaction.

AND NEVER HESITATE to call emergency services, MINUTES COUNT!

Lastly, be mindful of your personal conduct, even the smallest prank or lapse in judgment may prove very harmful to one of your guests.

FOOD ALLERGY SAFE HANDLING RESPONSIBILITIES OF THE MANAGER

The manager is the focal point for the food allergy safe handling program in any organization. They are the "go to" person for the entire facility. Their role is to:

Guest Focus

1. Never view guests with food allergies as picky or difficult. Remember food allergies, intolerances and sensitivities can be and are life threatening.

2. When speaking to the guest about their food issues listen carefully and take notes. Many times the guest will be very helpful in helping you and the chef determine easy food selection alternatives.

3. Be honest with your guest, if you **DON'T KNOW** something tell them. Do not guess, if you are wrong they are sick or dead.

4. Always believe the guest when they tell you they have a food issue. Once informed by a guest of a food allergy issue, think about what other sources in your establishment may cause a reaction.

5. Listen carefully to any guest who asks you to hold something on a dish. Be sure the hold is a preference not an allergy. Some guests will merely ask you to hold something rather than disclose the allergy.

FOOD ALLERGY SAFE HANDLING RESPONSIBILITIES OF THE MANAGER

6. Be sure to let your guest requiring food special handling know if the kitchen is overwhelmed and if a particular dish is likely to be mishandled, steer them toward something safer. Most guests will thank you for it!

As the Manager

1. Take charge when a guest informs your staff of a food allergy, intolerance or sensitivity.

2. Inform your team you have someone with a food allergy issue. This forewarns others of a special handling order and allows others to focus on your food allergy safe protocols, policies and procedures.

3. Consult with the chef and the guest to determine a safe selection.

4. Follow the guest's selection from order entry to delivery.

5. After the table is served allow the guest to inspect and review the plate. Don't leave until the dish has been approved. If there is a problem this enables you to respond immediately.

Back of the House

1. Once you are clear about the guest's food issue speak to the chef and your prep staff before making menu recommendations. Remember recipes and ingredients may have been changed for the day due to unavailability of standard ingredients and you may not be aware of the change. This is vitally important for your daily specials and any other "special" that may not be a part of your recipe book.

2. Always put the allergen on the kitchen order even if the guest is not ordering something with the allergen in it. This will prevent accidental contamination from something in the kitchen and it warns the kitchen in case there is a hidden allergen in something ordered.

3. Never just put "hold the _____." Always add the ALLERGY ALERT on the order. The kitchen has no way of knowing if this guest has an allergy or simply doesn't care for the ingredient. This exposes the guest to direct and cross contamination.

4. Always noticeably mark or flag the order and the allergen. This will allow the special handling order to stick out from all of the other orders.

5. Let the kitchen know the special handling order is coming. If you have to, as the manager, YOU, inform the kitchen. Some kitchens prohibit or limit call-in or verbal instructions from the floor staff.

FOOD ALLERGY SAFE HANDLING RESPONSIBILITIES OF THE MANAGER

6. Be sure you work out with the floor staff and the kitchen staff a segregated place to pick up the order and who will deliver it to the table. Be sure everyone knows not to touch or handle the order unless instructed to do so. This will prevent spills, splatters, steam, vapor, bumping and hand cross contamination.

7. Be sure to let your expeditor know you have a special handling order and who will be picking the order up.

8. If the special order contains the allergen or has become cross contaminated IT MUST BE REFIRED. Under no circumstances pick out, scrape off, wipe off or remove the allergen. Do not allow anyone else to do so either. DO NOT SERVE THE DISH UNTIL IT IS REMADE. Remember even the tiniest amount of the allergen can trigger a life threatening reaction. If there is an issue with the remake, YOU as the manager handle it. Your guests place their trust in you, you must protect them!

9. Always deliver the special order separately from all other plates, including the rest of the order on the table. Be sure if a tray is used that the tray has been thoroughly cleaned with a fresh cloth from the sanitizer bucket and that there is nothing else on the tray other than the special handling plate. This will prevent cross contamination from other dishes that might splash, spill or touch the order.

- Be aware of what is in your establishment and how it is handled. If you see something directly or cross contaminated remove it immediately.

- Know and understand your organization's food allergy safe handling protocols, procedures and processes.

- Make sure there is some reference point where staff can check for accurate food ingredients.

- Establish your organization's allergy safe food handling protocols, policies and procedures.

- Maintain, review and update the protocols, policies and procedures as required.

- Stay current with allergy safe food handling issues.

- Ensure all staff is trained in allergy safe food handling methods.

- Make sure all staff is clear on how to handle food allergy meal selection, meal preparation and meal service.

- Establish clear instructions on how to handle a food allergy reaction emergency.

FOOD ALLERGY SAFE HANDLING RESPONSIBILITIES OF THE MANAGER

- Ensure staff compliance with allergy safe food handling protocols, policies and procedures.

- Create a team approach to allergy safe food handling.

- Create an environment where staff is encouraged to suggest improvements to the protocols, policies and procedures.

- Create an environment where, in the event of a mistake, staff will do the right thing rather than cover it up.

- Create a safe and welcoming environment for food-challenged guests.

Our industry is seeing increased lawsuits, insurance claims and public complaints. Our liability becomes greater as law makers, courts and the public demand we educate our staff and implement protocols, policies and procedures to safeguard our guests.

We must protect the health and welfare of our guests. We must move to limit the liability of our staff and the establishment, and contribute to the success of all by proactively addressing this critical issue.

Allergy Reactions

- In case of a food allergy reaction, **always call** 911 or your emergency services.

- Know the address and phone number of the restaurant and be sure to tell them it is a suspected food allergy reaction.

- Remember in a crisis we tend to become flustered and may forget simple things like the address and phone number, so have a cheat sheet posted or clearly visible near the phone.

- Letting emergency services know that it is a suspected food allergy reaction will allow them to dispatch the appropriate personnel. Not all emergency personnel carry or are authorized to administer the drugs necessary to combat the reaction.

AND NEVER HESITATE to call emergency services, MINUTES COUNT!

Lastly, be mindful of your personal conduct, even the smallest prank or lapse in judgment may prove very harmful to one of your guests.

COMMON SOURCES OF FOOD ALLERGY CONTAMINATION

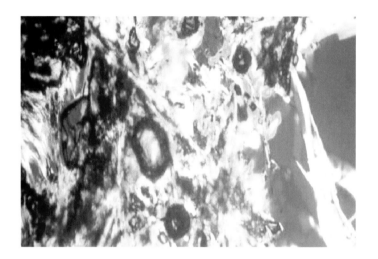

Improperly cleaned:

    a. tables, chairs, booths, benches
    b. condiments & containers
    c. table decorations
    d. menus
    e. check presentation folders
    f. trays

Publicly handled items like:

    a. crayons
    b. candy in candy dishes
    c. buffet utensils & buffet's service items
    d. salad bars, etc.

Storage and packaging, for example:

    a. pastry trays
    b. pie and cake cases
    c. walk-in storage
    d. multiple-use containers

1. Using one utensil to transfer multiple food items without washing/sanitizing in between each transfer.

2. Reusing kitchen equipment for multiple foods without washing and sanitizing. Offending equipment includes:
    a. food processors
    b. slicers
    c. mixers, blenders
    d. can openers, etc.

COMMON SOURCES OF FOOD ALLERGY CONTAMINATION

3. Cooking and holding equipment that is used for multiple foods such as:
    a. deep fryers
    b. char broilers
    c. flattops
    d. ovens
    e. broilers
    f. steam tables
    g. woks, etc.

4. Cooking implements used for multiple food without washing and sanitizing between each food such as
    a. cookie sheets
    b. hotel pans, pots & pans
    c. spatulas, forks, spoons, tongs & soup ladles
    d. thermometers, etc.
    e. mixing bowls
    f. sizzle platters
    g. rolling pins

5. Removing an allergen rather than remaking the dish.

6. Bad information imparted to the guest.

7. **Believing an allergy to be a preference.**

8. Poor communication between staff.

9. Using prep and staging surfaces for multiple foods without washing and sanitizing between each food.

10. **Aprons and apron pockets used to carry food containers.**

11. Cleaning/wipe clothes used multiple times without sanitizing.

12. Gloves used on multiple foods without changing them.

13. **Improperly cleaned spills such as milk on seats, carpets and other surfaces.**

14. Wiping off the edges of plates with a previously used unsanitized cloth.

15. Food transfer such as bits of one food dropping into another on steam tables or cold tables.

16. Vapor or splatter-off of steaming dishes or sizzling platters.

17. Poor description of dishes on menus.

18. Multiple food dredging bowls and pans.

19. Flour dust or crumbs on plates, utensils, cooking surfaces, staging and prep surfaces.

20. Multiple food cooking oils.

21. Multiple food pasta cookers.

22. Spilling, dripping, touching, vapor, or splattering on other plates in service windows.

23. Carrying multiple plates on the same tray as a special handling order.

24. Improperly cleaned service trays.

25. Accidentally dropping something into a cooking pot.

26. Refilling serving containers without washing and sanitizing them first.

27. Mixing multiple salads in the same bowl without washing and sanitizing between each use.

28. Garnishes touched, splattered, dripped or spilled on by a contaminate.

29. Outsides of cups, glasses, bowls, saucers plates utensils, place mats, and napkins, etc., that have come in contact with allergens.

30. When replenishing food **laying the serving utensil in another food.**

31. **Using a substitute ingredient in a recipe.**

32. Using a prepared food or ingredient whose recipe has changed.

33. Unexpected or hidden allergens such as flour on frozen french fries.

34. **Undisclosed secret recipes or ingredients.**

35. Improperly entered special handling orders.

CRITICAL ELEMENTS OF A SUCCESSFUL
FOOD ALLERGY SAFETY PROGRAM

It is important for each organization to create their own Food Allergy Safe Program based on the unique features of their operation. In creating such a program there are certain elements that are critical to the success of each. These elements are designed to aid each operation with a general framework by which they may design and customize their own successful Food Allergy Safe Program.

Policy

- Make sure all employees know and understand that food allergies, intolerances and sensitivities are not preferences and at best they make our guests ill; at worst they kill them.

- Instill in all employees that they are to believe a guest when they are informed of a food issue.

- Encourage them to listen carefully to the guest and take notes so they can effectively communicate their needs to others involved in their food preparation.

- Post somewhere visible to all employees the "Big 8 Allergens & Sesame."

- Be clear in your chain of command, who is informed and who is to be involved in the handling of these guests and their orders.

Protocol

1. Be sure all employees know how to clean, setup, and serve food-challenged guests.

2. Emphasize that no one is to suggest menu items to a food-challenged guest without first consulting with your food allergy expert on duty.

3. Encourage your employees to admit to the customer when they don't know something and never just guess.

4. Make sure allergy alerts are clearly visible and easily identifiable and always placed on orders whether the guest is ordering a food that contains the allergen or not.

5. Be consistent with how allergy alerts are handled and notated on reservations, dine-in and take-out orders.

6. Require all special handling orders to be remade when returned by the food-challenged guest.

CRITICAL ELEMENTS OF A SUCCESSFUL
FOOD ALLERGY SAFETY PROGRAM

Procedure

1. Encourage all employees to be constantly vigilant in the preparation and service of all food to avoid cross contamination.

2. Establish a consistent handling procedure in the kitchen for special food-challenged guest orders and a special place for these orders to be set and picked up by the designated employee.

3. Help employees recognize all potential sources of food-challenged guest exposure to allergens.

4. Have a consistent place for authorized personnel to reference ingredients in your menu items.

5. Make it easy for employees to report and act on witnessed contamination or cross contamination of foods or implements.

6. Be sure all employees know what to do when a food-challenged guest is having a reaction.
   a. In case of a food allergy reaction, always call 911 or your emergency services.
   b. Know the address and phone number of the restaurant and be sure to tell them it is a suspected food allergy reaction.
   c. Remember in a crisis we tend to become flustered and may forget simple things like the address and phone number, so have a cheat sheet posted or clearly visible near the phone.

7. Have a procedure to investigate reported allergen exposures.

8. Be sure everyone knows who to ask when they have a special food handling issue.

9. Be sure you have a system to inform all of your employees when ingredients change or have been substituted. Discourage substitutions unless the change is permanent.

10. Establish a procedure to regularly review the labels on the foods you purchase from purveyors.

11. Review policies, protocols and procedures frequently with all staff.

Keep current with the changes in our industry with regard to food allergy issues.

Food Allergy Safe
References & Resources

Food Allergies, The Putman Publishing Group 1987
By Neil S. Orenstein, Ph.D., and Sarah L. Bringham, M. S.

Food Allergies, Enjoying life with severe food allergy. Class Publishing Second edition 2007
By Tanya Wright   Medical Advisor: Dr. Joanne Clough

Food Allergies for Dummies, Wiley Publishing 2007
By Robert A. Wood, MD

The Food Allergy & Anaphylaxis Network
11781 Lee Jackson Highway, Suite 160
Fairfax, VA 22033-3309

Food to Some Poison to Others, Frederick Fell Publishers, inc. 2008
By Terry Traub R.D.H., B.H.

In Defense of Food, The Penguin Press 2008
By Michael Pollan

Techniques of Healthy Cooking, John Wiley & Sons, Inc. 2007
By The Culinary Institute of America

The Complete Food Allergy Cookbook, Three Rivers Press 1996
By Marilyn Gioannini

The Omnivore's Dilemma, The Penguin Press 2007
By Michael Pollan

FOOD ALLERGY SAFE TRAINER'S GUIDE

The purpose of the trainer's guide is to provide an overview of the process necessary to instruct your staff for allergy safe food handling. It is important to have a strong working knowledge of the corresponding training manual as well as an equally strong working knowledge of your operation. The manual is designed to create **TOP OF MIND** for a comprehensive general knowledge of allergy safe food handling. However, as a trainer for your organization you are free to customize the presentation to fit your organization's specific operation.

Any training program is improved by participant interaction. This provides the trainer and participants with unique insights into the level of knowledge of their staff and an appreciation for the challenges they face each day. It is important to encourage input from participants to allow each the opportunity to be a part of your allergy safe food handling solution.

As a trainer you may become privy to information not normally shared. Be sure not to be judgmental and remember this is your opportunity to dispel individual myths and misconceptions your staff may have regarding allergy safe food handling.

Finally, the creation of a team approach to allergy safe food handling will maximize the effectiveness of your program. The more effective your program the safer and therefore more welcoming your establishment to your food-challenged guests.

GENERAL TRAINING TIPS

A. Have participants turn off cell phones and anything else that may create a distraction.

B. When possible hold the class away from the work place to avoid interruption.

C. Stick to your time table as much as possible.

D. Give frequent breaks and always have a full hour for lunch, remember the mind will only absorb what the backside can withstand.

E. Involve the class directly as much as possible.

F. Keep discussions on point.

G. Ask questions about their experiences or observations on subjects such as:

- Do they or someone they know have food challenges?
- How does it affect their lives?
- How does it affect their decisions and choices?
- What do they do about their food challenges?
- How do they handle them?
- Have they encountered guests with food allergies?
- How did they handle the guest?
- What areas do they see posing potential food allergy hazards?
- What do they do daily in their jobs to prevent food allergy contamination?

- What would they change if they could that would make things safer?
- Have they worked other places that had a Food Allergy Safe program?
- What was effective or ineffective about their program?
- What do they see as their role in guest food allergy safety?
- What do they perceive is the impact of not following Food Allergy Safe policies, procedures and protocols?
- How can each of them create TOP OF MIND in their own jobs and environments for food allergy safety issues?

H. Ask for input and ideas in each section. This will help you identify specific areas in your organization that you may wish to address company wide.

I. Stress it takes **everyone** to make a Food Allergy Safe program effective.

J. Ask for each person's commitment to guest safety and encourage their ongoing contributions to your organization's Food Allergy Safe handling program.

INTRODUCTION

Emphasize:

A. More individuals eat away from home due to busy life styles.
- This increases the opportunity for accidental exposure to allergens and makes the guest more vulnerable to our mistakes.

B. The scientific communities' statistical estimates of food allergy issues.
- The number of people made ill or killed each year.
- The fact that these cases are known to be under reported.

C. The problem is growing.
- Food allergies are the leading cause for allergic reaction based emergency room visits.
- Rising medical costs.

D. Our responsibility as an industry to do our part to be part of the solution.

E. The increased liability food allergy issues pose to our industry, our organizations, our jobs and our reputations.

WHY THIS TRAINING IS IMPORTANT TO MY ORGANIZATION AND TO ME?

Emphasize:

A. 2 out of every 10 people have some sort of food issue.
- Our opportunity to contribute to public health.
- Creation of a safe dining environment.

B. A safe establishment welcomes food-challenged guests.
- Lack of accommodation turns business away.

C. What studies show when we are able to accommodate food-challenged guests.

- How this benefits the guest.
- How this benefits the business.
- How this benefits the employees.
- How this benefits the public.

D. The quote reveals how professionals in our industry view the issue.

E. How this training makes each employee more valuable.

F. What a Food Allergy Safe Certified team means to the industry, the guest, the establishment and to themselves.

FOOD ALLERGY LAWS AND REGULATIONS

Emphasize:

A. Food Allergy Labeling and Consumer Protection Act, FDA Food Code, Sabrina's Law

- What they are.
- Why they came about.
- How they came about.
- Explain the history and progression of each.
- When and why they became mandatory.

B. The general purpose, meaning and the ultimate impact of each law on:

- The industry
- The individual establishment
- The employee
- The guest
- Present and future state Legislation

C. What will happen if our industry does not comply.

WHAT IS A FOOD ALLERGY?

Emphasize:

A. Define food allergy.

- Why it affects the body?
- How it affects the body?
- What happens with repeated exposure.

B. Describe food allergy reactions.

- Mild – What are the symptoms.
- Severe – Define Anaphylaxis
  — What the general symptoms are.

— What the consequences of anaphylaxis are.

— The number of people that are estimated to be hospitalized each year.

C. Define food intolerances and sensitivities.

- What the range of symptoms are.
- What the symptoms are.

D. Define celiac disease.

- What it is.
- What causes it.
- Where gluten is found.
- What the disease symptoms are.
- What the long-term impact of the disease is.
- Explain that the disease is ultimately fatal if there is continued gluten exposure.

E. There is no cure for food allergies, intolerances, sensitivities or celiac disease.

- What the only known treatment is.
- What can cause reactions in allergy sensitive people.
- How quickly reaction can begin.
- How long each reaction can last.
- How long individuals could stay in the hospital.
- How long people suffer from the effects of each reaction and what the long-term effects can be.
- What the financial impact is to the individual.
- That there is no way to measure the mental toll reactions take.

F. How many people will seek medical aid annually.

- How many go to emergency rooms.
- How many will die.
- How many seek private medical aid.
- Discuss the fact of how many people will seek medical aid annually.
- Discuss that the number of people impacted is under reported.
- Quote how many emergency rooms in the U.S.
- Call attention to the fact that we don't know how many people self treat.

G. How many people are affected by food allergies.

- Quote Center for Disease Control (CDC), medical professionals and the scientific communities' percentages.

H. How many people are affected by food intolerances and/or sensitivities.
- Quote medical professionals and the scientific communities percentages.
- Quote U.S. population.
- Quote estimated numbers affected.
- Cite that many individuals will have issues with more than one food.

I. How food issues impact individuals daily lives.
- Where they eat.
- Where they shop.
- What events they attend.
- Where they vacation.
- Where they stay.
- What schools or day care facilities they use.
- What form of transportation they use.
- What they do when they identify a Food Allergy Safe establishment.

J. What the major allergens are.
- That the "Big 8 Allergens & Sesame" are the focus of the Food Labeling and Consumer Protection Act and Sabrina's Law.
- What percentage of allergic reactions they account for.

K. Other names and hidden sources of the "Big 8 Allergens & Sesame."
- Go over the various names.
- Review where they can be found.
- Stress the list cannot include all items.
- Stress they must read labels.
- What the major component that causes the reaction is.
- What will not eliminate the offending component.
- What will eliminate offending component.
- The additional ways proteins can be transmitted.

CASE STUDIES

Emphasize:
A. Background
- Who the subject is.
- What their history/background is.
- What their allergy is.
- How the allergy was diagnosed.
- How they handle their allergy.

B. Event
- What happened.
- How the reaction progressed.
- What actions were taken.
- How the exposure was investigated.
- How the exposure was determined.
- What was the ultimate cause of contamination or exposure.

C. The Consequence
- What was the personal impact to the victim.
- What was the personal impact to the victim's friends, family, etc.
- What was the financial impact.
- What was the impact to the establishment.
- What was the impact to the employees.
- What was the potential impact to others.

D. Group Discussion
1. Talk about how and why the exposure occurred.
2. How exposure could have been prevented.
3. What your policies, procedures and protocols are or should be to prevent a similar situation.
4. The role of each employee to prevent the exposure.
5. The potential and real liability of the business, the management and the employee.
6. The potential and real impact this liability has on the business, the management and employee in terms of:
   a. Legal exposure
   b. Financial loss
   c. Loss of job
   d. Closure of the business
   e. Impact on their respective reputations
   f. Public perception
   g. Emotional, mental and physical tolls
7. Most importantly, discuss the impact or potential impact on the victim such as:
   a. Loss of life
   b. Permanent physical damage
   c. Financial
   d. Loss of work or job
   e. Impact to their business
   f. Loss of one time experiences, such as vacations, business trips, etc.

g. Emotional, mental and physical tolls

h. Impact on family, friends, business associates, etc.

8. Discuss the impact that the smallest oversight or deviation from policy, procedure and protocol can have.

RESPONSIBILITIES of: the INDIVIDUAL, HOST OR HOSTESS, BUS PERSON, SERVER, DISH WASHER, CHEF or COOK & the MANAGER

Emphasize:

A. The role in and how each position effects your Food Allergy Safe Handling:

- Policies

- Procedures

- Protocols

B. Cover and review all points in every section for each position heading.

C. Stress the program is a team effort and all must be diligent.

D. No one person alone will make a Food Allergy Safe Program effective.

E. Food allergies, intolerances and sensitivities are not preferences but serious medical conditions.

F. How to react in an emergency.

G. Point out the importance of personal conduct and the lack thereof, creates potential dangers to the public.

COMMON SOURCES OF FOOD ALLERGY CONTAMINATION

A. Cover each section point by point.

B. Discuss how each of these items can be involved in contamination.

C. The individual's role in preventing contamination through proper use and cleaning.

D. Give examples of how items become contaminated.

E. Be sure to ask for input from the class, they will provide additional areas of concern specific to your operation.

CRITICAL ELEMENTS OF A SUCCESSFUL FOOD ALLERGY SAFE PROGRAM

A. Talk about the general requirements and the purpose of your Food Allergy Safe Program:

- Policies

- Procedures

- Protocols

B. Explain why these elements are critical to your program.

CERTIFICATION

Individual

- To complete the certification process each individual needs to take and pass the exam.

- To take the exam, go to www.allergysafecert.com and follow instructions on the website.

- When you have completed registration and successfully passed the exam your personal certification card will be mailed to you within 30 days.

- Your certification is valid for three years.

- The certification belongs to you as an individual and should be presented and copied by each employer.

Employer

- As an employer, when 80% of your staff is Allergy Safe Certified you can apply for site certification.

- To apply for site certification, go to www.allergysafecert.com and follow instructions on the website.

- When your site certification registration is completed an Allergy Safe Certified door/window sticker and reproducible Allergy Safe Certified logo will be provided within 30 days.

- Your site certification is valid for one year.

ALLERGY SAFE BASIC TRAINING PROGRAM TRAINING GUIDE

Section I – Introduction

Before you begin the presentation emphasize:

1. 2 Out of every 10 guests will have some sort of food issue, which they may or may not declare to us voluntarily.
2. How important food allergy safety is to your organization.
3. The impact it can have on the guest, employees and the business.
4. Food allergy safety is a team effort.
5. It is part of food safety codes and the subject of public laws.

Section II – Recap after Slide 15

1. Food allergies can and do kill, sensitivities and intolerances can and do cause permanent physical damage.
2. There is currently no cure for food allergies.
3. The only way to keep a food allergy individual safe is no contact with the allergen.
4. 0 Parts per million is the only acceptable level of allergen in any dish.
5. Heat and cold do not destroy allergens, only residue removal through washing and sanitizing.

Section III – Recap after slide 26

1. Employees are responsible for memorizing all the big 8 allergens and should know sesame for our canadian guests.
2. The number 1 allergy in children is milk and eggs are number 2.
3. Employees should familiarize themselves with the products in their area that may contain big 8 allergens and sesame.
4. Discuss with trainees who and where in your facility they can check for food allergens in your foods.
5. Remind them to think about possible food allergens in beverages and condiments.

Section IV – Recap after slide 36

1. To prevent accidental contamination food allergy alerts must go on everything attached to an order, from kitchen tickets to banquet orders and prep orders – even if the individual has ordered around the allergy.
2. Treat all intolerances and sensitivities as allergies.
3. Discuss your food allergy guest handling procedure.
4. Discuss whose responsibility it is in your organization to follow a food allergy order from start to finish.

5. Remind that inappropriate personal conduct can seriously injure or even cost a food allergy guest their life.

Section V – Recap after each position

Slide 37 begins the specific positions; share the individual section with all employees, after that go over only the positions that are represented by the trainees in your class.

Responsibilities of the individual

1. Always believe a guest when they tell you they have a food issue.
2. Never recommend menu items without consulting your pic or manager.
3. If you don't know if something is allergy safe say so and then find out.

Responsibilities of the host or hostess

1. Discuss your specific procedure for alerting the rest of the staff of a food allergy guest.
2. Point out the best tables to seat a food allergy guest.
3. Discuss your specific procedure for informing the rest of the staff of food allergy guests in a large party or event.
4. Discuss your specific procedure for taking reservations for a food allergy guest.

Responsibilities of bus personnel

1. Discuss if you have an allergy table set-up, where it is and how to restock it.
2. Discuss whom they should check with before bringing guest-requested items to a food allergy guest.
3. Emphasize they are not to recommend menu or drink selections to a food allergy guest.

Responsibilities of servers

1. Discuss your specific food allergy guest handling procedure.
2. Discuss who their go-to person on duty is for food allergy questions.
3. Discuss your specific pos food allergy entry procedure.
4. Emphasize all food allergy guest orders must have an allergy alert on them even if the guest has ordered around the allergen.
5. Discuss where in your kitchen food allergy orders can be picked up and who will deliver them to the table if it is not the server.
6. Emphasize food allergens cannot be scraped off, picked out, or wiped off, the dish must be remade.

ALLERGY SAFE BASIC TRAINING PROGRAM TRAINING GUIDE

Responsibilities of dishwashers

1. Discuss your policy for cleaning traps, drains, rinse water and clean side surfaces.
2. If your dishwashers sometimes pull items off salad bars, buffets, hot or cold lines or restocks any food items in your facility, be sure to discuss your allergy safe procedures as they pertain to these areas.
3. If your dishwashers sometimes perform prep duties, discuss your allergy safe kitchen procedures as they pertain to these areas.
4. Emphasize attention to their gloves, hands and surfaces when handling items for food allergy guests.

Responsibilities of chefs & cooks

1. Discuss who in your kitchen follows the food allergy order from start to finish.
2. Discuss whom in your facility the allergy experts on duty are.
3. Discuss your food allergy order preparation procedures.
4. Discuss specifically where food allergy orders are placed for pickup in your kitchen.
5. Discuss who specifically is responsible for reviewing product labels, and how often.
6. Discuss your specific policy for handling substitutions from purveyors.
7. Discuss your specific policy on recipe substitutions.
8. Discuss how you specifically communicate recipe substitutions and changes to all staff and who is responsible for the communication.
9. Discuss where to look or who to ask about food allergens in your foods if their usual expert is not available.

Section VI – After slide 70 recap

1. Discuss your company's policy and procedure for reporting and investigating any food allergy reaction incident.
2. Discuss your company's policy and procedure for reporting and removing items that become contaminated or cross contaminated with a food allergen.
3. Emphasize your company's commitment to remake any dish and to pull any item that has been contaminated by a food allergen not belonging in that food item.

Section VII – After slide 79 recap

1. Multiple food cooking oils will transfer any food allergen that has entered the oil.
2. Vapor and steam can transfer food allergens.
3. Crumbs and dust (especially flours and peanut shells) can be a source of food allergy contamination and cross contamination.

4. Can openers, cookie sheets, rolling pins, meat slicers and other multiple foods use items between washing and sanitizing can be sources of food allergy contamination.

5. Remember heat does not kill food allergens, so multiple foods' cooking surfaces are sources of food allergy contamination.

6. Remember there is no such thing as a secret ingredient.

Section VIII – After the very last slide conclusion

1. Discuss with all employees what they are to do in the event of a guest food allergy reaction. Be sure they know where your phone number and address are posted so they can direct emergency personnel to your location.

2. Close with reemphasizing that you have food allergy policies, procedures and protocols and they are required to follow them as part of your food safety program. Let them know the ramifications to your guests, employees, business and their continued employment if they don't.